Cambridge Elements

Elements in Race in American Literature and Culture
edited by
John Ernest
University of Delaware
Stephanie Li
Duke University

RACE CLASS

Reading Mexican American Literature in the Era of Neoliberalism, 1981–1984

José Antonio Arellano
United States Air Force Academy

Shaftesbury Road, Cambridge CB2 8EA, United Kingdom

One Liberty Plaza, 20th Floor, New York, NY 10006, USA

477 Williamstown Road, Port Melbourne, VIC 3207, Australia

314–321, 3rd Floor, Plot 3, Splendor Forum, Jasola District Centre, New Delhi – 110025, India

103 Penang Road, #05–06/07, Visioncrest Commercial, Singapore 238467

Cambridge University Press is part of Cambridge University Press & Assessment, a department of the University of Cambridge.

We share the University's mission to contribute to society through the pursuit of education, learning and research at the highest international levels of excellence.

www.cambridge.org
Information on this title: www.cambridge.org/9781009532938

DOI: 10.1017/9781009429566

© José Antonio Arellano 2025

This publication is in copyright. Subject to statutory exception and to the provisions of relevant collective licensing agreements, no reproduction of any part may take place without the written permission of Cambridge University Press & Assessment.

When citing this work, please include a reference to the DOI 10.1017/9781009429566

First published 2025

A catalogue record for this publication is available from the British Library

ISBN 978-1-009-53293-8 Hardback
ISBN 978-1-009-42954-2 Paperback
ISSN 2753-6343 (online)
ISSN 2753-6335 (print)

Cambridge University Press & Assessment has no responsibility for the persistence or accuracy of URLs for external or third-party internet websites referred to in this publication and does not guarantee that any content on such websites is, or will remain, accurate or appropriate.

For EU product safety concerns, contact us at Calle de José Abascal, 56, 1°, 28003 Madrid, Spain, or email eugpsr@cambridge.org

Race Class

Reading Mexican American Literature in the Era of Neoliberalism, 1981–1984

Elements in Race in American Literature and Culture

DOI: 10.1017/9781009429566
First published online: December 2025

José Antonio Arellano
United States Air Force Academy
Author for correspondence: José Antonio Arellano,
joseantonio.arellano@gmail.com

Abstract: *Race Class* identifies two competing aesthetics, the "recognitional" and the "redistributive," that developed in Mexican American literature during the 1980s. Recognitional literature seeks to express an ethnic identity via a circular narratological discourse of self-creation. This expressive view of literature fosters readerly sympathy via testimony and textual personification, the author argues, but ultimately forecloses interpretive judgment. Redistributive literature instead averts the readers' sympathy to produce the evaluative distance through which interpretative judgment and structural critique are enabled. By tracking these competing aesthetics, *Race Class* shows why the Chicano Movement should not be understood as a working-class enterprise, why higher education cannot be a mechanism of social justice, and why the left continues to misunderstand the nature of economic inequality today.

Keywords: Chicano, literature, race, class, history

© José Antonio Arellano 2025
ISBNs: 9781009532938 (HB), 9781009429542 (PB), 9781009429566 (OC)
ISSNs: 2753-6343 (online), 2753-6335 (print)

Contents

1. Introduction — 1
2. The Development of Chicano Literature and Culture — 13
3. The Limits of the Chicano Solution — 16
4. A Critique of Chicano Activism and Literature: Richard Rodriguez *Hunger of Memory* (1982) — 22
5. Recognitional Witnessing versus Redistributive Representation: *I, Rigoberta Menchú* (1984) — 31
6. Identifying the Enemy: Daniel James *Famous All Over Town* (1983) — 37
7. Recognitional Novels: Arturo Islas *The Rain God* (1984) — 43
8. The Culture of Poverty and the Program Era: Sandra Cisneros *The House on Mango Street* (1984) — 50
9. Against Literature? The Redistributive within *The House on Mango Street* — 59
10. Conclusion: On Trying to Get It Right — 65

Works Cited — 67

1 Introduction

The title *Race Class* is meant to invoke the literature classroom, understood as one of the premier American sites where conversations about race and class take place.[1] I have in mind a scene like one represented in Daniel James' 1983 novel *Famous All Over Town*, wherein a junior high school teacher assigns a novel to her students. During a class discussion, she asks the students, "Why is it we really need to read well and easily?" (74), a question that becomes more specific as she guides the conversation away from the practical answers offered by the students toward her didactic ones concerning their identity. Although their initial responses include such pragmatic thoughts as, "so we can get to college and make money" and "[so] we [can] buy stuff at the store," the teacher instead highlights how the characters in the novel are "Mexican-American young people like so many of us here. We can identify with them, can we not? And learn from their experience" (75). The question she is asking, then, is not simply, Why should students read well and easily? but, rather, Why should students read fiction about Mexican Americans?

This self-reflexive moment was not unique at the time. The question of why one should read and create Mexican American literature appears in some of the most significant works published in the early 1980s. These writers did not take as givens the answers provided by the Chicano generation of the mid-1960s and 1970s.[2] For that older Chicano generation, the incorporation of literature about Mexican Americans into the classroom was a crucial step toward self-liberation.[3] In their view, Mexican American literature would dispel the false notions of inferiority that were fostered in the so-called "Mexican Schools."

---

[1] The term "race," though, tends to be a stand-in for "ethnicity" and "culture." As Kwame Anthony Appiah notes, "The truth is that there are no races: there is nothing in the word that can do all we ask race to do for us" (45). Appiah is not suggesting that there is no such thing as racism, of course, but he does argue against the term's continued reification within academia. Karen E. Fields and Barbara J. Fields also remind us of the debunked nineteenth-century scientism (what they call "bio-racism") that gave rise to the idea of biological entities called "races." They write, "Race in today's biology is not a traditionally named group of people but a statistically defined population" (4–5). Like Appiah, the Fieldses argue against the continued reification of the concept treated independently from the historical conditions that give rise to racism; discussions of race independent of the political economy obscure the causes of inequality. For an elaboration of this point, see Barbara Fields, "Slavery, Race, and Ideology in the United States of America," republished in *Racecraft* (111–148). It is more common today to refer to one's "culture" than one's "race." For an account of how the former continues to reify the latter, see Walter Benn Michaels' "Race Into Culture: A Critical Genealogy of Cultural Identity."

[2] The term "Chicano" was used in the early twentieth century as a pejorative term but was reclaimed by Mexican American activists during the 1960s and 1970s to indicate a collective sense of pride among Mexican Americans. I use the historical term "Chicano" to refer to the late 1960s and 1970s Chicano Movement and its participants. Contemporary Chicana/o/xs tend to use more inclusive language to avoid the lexical genders of Spanish nouns

[3] For example, see Philip D. Ortego y Gasca 296.

With the increased migration of Mexicans into the United States, public school systems established segregated curricula that "stressed vocational over academic instruction" (García and Castro 11). According to Mario T. García and Sal Castro, in the early Mexican Schools, "students were given over four hours of trade instruction and only an hour and a half of academic instruction" (11).[4] These conditions led to the development of the Chicano Civil Rights Movement, galvanized by the 1968 high school student "walkouts" (or "blowouts"). Students demanded more Chicano representation on the teaching faculty and in the studied content. They asserted that content by and about Mexican Americans could counteract the problems they faced by promoting self-pride and portraying a more complex, antiracist portrait of Mexican American lives.

In *Famous*, however, readers see a different situation. Published in 1983, the novel depicts a supportive Jewish counselor who appears to have learned the lessons of the Chicano Civil Rights Movement. He knows that "every youngster with a Mexican name gets shunted into Metal Shop or Carpentry" (66). Having grown up in a hostile antisemitic environment, the counselor understands the value of cultural pride and encourages the fourteen-year-old protagonist, Rudy "Chato" Medina, to learn about his ethnicity, develop his sense of self, and carve a path through college to the middle class (205). Moreover, Chato's English teacher preaches the value of democratic inclusion, assigning a novel whose plot and setting appear similar to Chato's life (74). This novel is summarized by Chato as being about "a certain Mexican kid named Pancho which [sic] his father worked for the railroad and his sister Maria cleaned house for rich old ladies" (70). Compare this plot to *Famous*, which is about a boy called Chato whose father works for the railroad and whose sister works in a factory. Yet Chato, who has the most in common with the assigned novel's protagonist, finds the novel pedantic, while a classmate points out how a young woman in the story is, as she puts it, "working and I wish I was" (75). If, for Chato's teacher, the importance of reading about Mexican Americans is connected to the value of developing one's ethnicity, this scene exposes economic class as the gulf the students do not traverse via identity.

Famous, through the students' responses, presents a view of literature understood as the gateway to upward-class mobility and literacy as its key. Reading "well" and "easily" implies linguistic fluency and social dexterity. Via the teacher's guidance, however, the novel depicts a competing didactic view of literary fluency understood as the pathway to developing their character. For the teacher, the characters' ethnicity is the relevant fact facilitating such learning.

---

[4] According to García and Castro, students were "encouraged or forced to work with their hands in shop classes" as a way of developing an easily exploited source of cheap labor (11). See José Antonio Villarreal *Pocho* (1959) for a literary example of this problem.

Famous may appear to present these views of the value of reading literature as divergent; however, as I make clear in Section 6, its plot will expose their homology.[5] The novel dramatizes the convergence of these narratives to show the dynamic of their confluence, thereby exposing to readers the potential attraction to narratives of class mobility ("get to college and make money") and narratives of identity ("we can identify with them [...] and learn from their experience"). This self-reflexive scene can thus produce the ironic distance through which readers can evaluate their own motivations for reading this kind of novel, including, perhaps, one's desire for a kind of relative readerly "ease." Insofar as one could describe the value of Mexican American literature as enabling self-development through ethnic identification, it is a value that the novel's classroom scene prevents.

Famous dramatizes the question, Wherefore Mexican American literature? precisely when, during the 1980s, divergent answers to this question were being worked out. If other texts had circulated narratives that foreground identity (the authors' and characters'), *Famous* instead invites its readers to question their own assumptions regarding the value of studying ethnic literature. This invitation, though, has been virtually ignored because the novel was written by a white man named Daniel James, who hid his real name and used the pseudonym Danny Santiago to publish a novel about Mexican Americans.[6] James' father was a wealthy businessman whose considerable fortune afforded James an education at the prestigious Phillips Academy and Yale, not to mention the commission of the famed architect Charles Sumner Greene to design their home in the Carmel Highlands (purchased in 2022 by Brad Pitt for $40 million). James is not only *not* a Chicano, but he also appears to embody their very enemy by being a privileged white male who can exploit their lives for his benefit.

In what follows, however, I show how *Famous* participates in a legacy of modernism that makes available an aesthetic that explicitly demands our interpretive judgment instead of facilitating our sympathetic identification. James foregrounds the very features that constitute novels and the pedagogical tools enabling their classroom use. "Like always," notices Chato, the assignment to read a novel's chapter comes with "ten questions," including, "Can you find a good example of foreshadowing in the pages you have just read?" (71). I can

---

[5] *Famous All Over Town* joins other novels of the early 1980s that similarly establish an initial tension between an identity plot (usually about protagonists learning to be proud of their heritage) and a plot of upward-class mobility. See José Antonio Villarreal's *Clemente Chacón* (1984).

[6] As John Gregory Dunn infamously disclosed a year after the novel's publication, "Danny Santiago, strictly speaking, is not his name. He is not a Chicano. Nor is he young. He is seventy-three years old. He is an Anglo. He is a graduate of Andover and Yale." Publishers were not interested in the novel until the 1980s. See James' ("Santiago's") "Danny Santiago Makes a Call on Daniel James."

imagine the discussions of themes and settings that are sure to follow, and the classroom activities – planned around the novel's assignable chapters – meant to highlight the specificity of characters, their social setting, and the subtle shifts in focalization. I can also imagine the ensuing questions from students concerning the very need to learn how to read literature at all: Why bother with any of it?

Those of my readers who teach literature might have experienced a similar scene as the one *Famous* depicts. Literature instructors perhaps understand the teacher's attempt to steer the discussion away from the supposed purchasing power of literacy toward loftier aspirations. Indeed, instructors might feel a more general sense of unease about their status within the professionalizing context of institutions of higher education embedded in an economic system that, by its motivating logic, must incentivize profit margins. Students seek credentials to enrich their lives, but what they mean by "enrichment" might differ from what instructors feel a study of literature as art could enable. When we consider the role of the humanities within higher education, the question, Why bother? feels especially urgent when the market-driven answers – "to make money" to "buy stuff at the store" – appear more relevant than ironic.

The professionalizing context of higher education thus compounds the problems motivating the question, Wherefore ethnic literary study? by raising questions concerning its *own* function.[7] One type of response this unease produces emphasizes literary study's political value. Although they disagree on the particulars, literary scholars – or literary *critics* as Joseph North would have it – describe the ability of literary studies to teach students how to reform democracy and develop a more just and inclusive society. North returns his readers to a time when, he argues, practicing "criticism" was understood as synonymous with learning to diagnose social ills and intervening to correct them (1–2). According to North, one can learn how to "cultivate" in students an oppositional stance toward "culture" and thereby "intervene" to disrupt the status quo (1–2). By cultivating students' "affective or aesthetic capabilities" (178), one might teach students to "analyz[e] the culture" and facilitate an "intervention" (17). Bruce Robbins takes North to task for failing to consider the primacy of identity in political interventions from "the resistance to racism and the Vietnam War to the vitality and persistence of the civil rights movement and the other movements that inspired it" (60). Like North, though, he also takes his readers to the past – in his case, the 1960s. During this time, Robbins argues, calls to include the study of ethnic literature within the context of higher

---

[7] Referring to the professionalizing context of higher education, John Guillory has recently argued, in *Professing Criticism*, that the tension between literary study's "disciplinary protocols" and "its identity as a profession" will persist, especially as one presents the professionalization of the discipline *as* the solution to one's unease (viii).

education were coterminous with concrete political reforms (130–132). The legacy of the post-1960s intervention could thus highlight how higher education created spaces "where contesting claims to representation are adjudicated and contesting versions of collectivity are fashioned, scrutinized, and tested out" (147). For Robbins, this careful consideration within literature classrooms remains vital to reform modes of governance, especially when the subjects in question are women, people of color, and other marginalized communities. So long as literary critics uphold this oppositional attitude toward the status quo, they will be seemingly working on behalf of justice.

In both accounts, it remains unclear how the dynamics of the reification of racial prejudice and the perpetuation of class inequality interact to maintain said status quo – other than "intersectionally."[8] But the specifics of this intersection matter; the diagnosis and the mode of intervention would change if students considered racism as a symptom of class inequality, or if class inequality was but one justification for continued racism. In Robbins' and North's accounts, though, terms including "opposition" and "intervention" are too often taken as givens. In the entirety of North's *Literary Criticism*, when looking for a concrete example of what he describes as the "cultivation of aesthetic sensibility" necessary for the cultivation of an oppositional stance, one can only find vague repetitions of his central idea: The study of literature provides "rigorous methods for analyzing the culture and for taking action to change it" (12). For Robbins, an ethnic body of work like Mexican American literature appears to be inherently oppositional, presumably because the status quo in question is that of white hegemony. But how might one begin to understand a status quo that involves the very work of higher education and literary study? Where do students of literature stand if the supposed oppositional nature of literary criticism is not only compatible with the politics of the status quo but is itself one of its engines?

Race Class is meant to contribute to these debates by highlighting the mistaken conflation of race and class and by refusing to play the justification

---

[8] Robbins provides a useful overview of the term *intersectionality*, noting its coinage by legal scholar Kimberlé Crenshaw in 1989, as well as its longer history with the 1974 Combahee River Collective (139). Crenshaw was instrumental in advancing Critical Race Theory in essays including "Race, Reform, and Retrenchment" and "Mapping the Margins." North comes closer to the untangling that *Race Class* calls for in relation to the term "intersectional." North provides a compelling set of questions that ask readers to consider the specificity of class in relation to questions of exploitation: "To what extent were second-wave feminist critiques of the welfare state likely to secure basic structural changes, and to what extent were they working to replace a materialist politics with a mere politics of recognition, thereby, serving, albeit often inadvertently, as the 'handmaidens of neoliberalism?' Which of the race critiques were genuinely challenging to the existing racial order, and which were in fact expressions of that racial order in its newly 'diverse,' 'multicultural,' and US-expansionist form?" (58–59).

game – wherein one must justify the enterprise of the study of literature by invoking terms outside of the enterprise itself.[9] If what one wants is, say, a political intervention, the literature classroom is, in principle, replaceable, or it proves to be useful insofar as it operates as a venue for indoctrination. I instead join John Guillory in arguing that "The study of literature is a rational procedure for what can be known about an object" (*Professing* 344), a study that is sufficiently interesting in itself to warrant our attention.[10] And yet, because literary critics and historians continue to mistakenly treat race and class as entangled proxies of each other, getting a better account of the literary texts in question could be understood *as* minimally political. So, although the politicization of literary study is not what motivates the following, the present historical conditions render the cognitive enterprise of literary critical understanding minimally political.[11]

Race Class provides a much-needed reinvigorated account of a few works from the early 1980s. I say "much needed" because most of the texts I analyze in what follows have been discussed (or ignored) for decades, rendering an ossified critical consensus. As I show in Section 3, the stakes of this mistaken critical consensus are apparent in the mischaracterization of the Chicano Movement and its aftermath as a working-class political enterprise. As I show in Section 4, whereas Robbins and North present an earlier 1960s generation as getting something fundamentally correct about the nature of political intervention and academic activism, for a writer like Richard Rodriguez, the 1960s liberals had mischaracterized a problem of class inequality as one of racial discrimination, such that anti-assimilation could be understood as anti-capitalism. Reevaluating Rodriguez's *Hunger of Memory* (1982) will help my readers understand how the left focused on higher education and initiatives for affirmative action, which, Rodriguez argued, benefited the upper classes while ignoring the economically vulnerable.

Rodriguez, though, has been considered "a foe to progressive Chicano/a politics," as José F. Aranda describes (24). According to John Alba Culter, *Hunger of*

---

[9] As Stanley Fish has repeated for decades, the game of justification can only end in the diminishment of the very integrity of the profession as such. See *Save The World on Your Own Time*.
[10] Stefan Collini summarizes this point in his review of John Guillory's *Professing Criticism*: "The study of literature is a rational procedure for what can be known about an object (the literary work). This is a cognitive enterprise, and it centres on the study of writing that is 'sufficiently wrought' for the writing itself to be of interest. Put in that simple way, this may seem to beg all the important questions, yet it also points to an intellectual achievement that should not be disregarded. This doesn't settle anything, for, as we know, justification is a never-ending game [...] but exaggerating the political consequences of what we do does not terminate that endless chain of questions and answers any better than any other claim" (5).
[11] My repeated qualification of this politics as "minimal" is meant to highlight a difference between academic politics and that of organizing and mobilizing. See the Introduction to Adolph Reed, Jr.'s *Class Notes*.

Memory evinces a "neoliberal ethos" (107). For Culter, novels such as Arturo Islas' *The Rain God* (1984) and Sandra Cisneros' *The House on Mango Street* (1984) offer a far more progressive political vision that counters Rodriguez's conservativism. This view does not acknowledge how novels like *The Rain God* and *The House on Mango Street* help produce the ideological support for an economic system that has only intensified since the time of their publication. And this insufficient characterization of Rodriguez fails to highlight how he offers a trenchant critique of the left's misguided attempts to counteract this system.

My claims may come as a surprise to my readers. As anyone who knows anything about Rodriguez will readily point out, Rodriguez has never identified himself as a progressive, nor, to my knowledge, has he claimed allegiance to the political left.[12] A graduate of Stanford, which he describes as "the school rich people went to" (139–140), and Columbia, part of the coveted Ivy League, Rodriguez has been the beneficiary of a prestigious education that enabled a distinguished writing career, one that materially separates his interests from those of the working class. Yet, to begin to spell out the case for reevaluating Rodriguez, at the height of neoliberalism's ascendance, it was he who charged the left for failing the "revolutionary demand" of "reform[ing] primary and secondary schools" and securing "good teachers ...with sufficient time to devote to individual students," and demanding "jobs and good housing ... three meals a day, in safe neighborhoods" (151–52). While such criticisms are easy to lob without having to produce a concrete alternative, Rodriguez does invoke the importance of collective bargaining for "unskilled" workers (116). He recalls how the positions available to his father in factories and canneries never offered the representation that would have advocated for job security and healthcare: "Nowhere a union" (116). And referring to the undocumented workers exploited by a system that used them as cheap labor, Rodriguez argued that they were "Persons apart. People lacking a union obviously, people without grounds" (149). He argues that the left's focus on higher education as the solution to the problem of labor conditions in the United States fundamentally ignores the reality of workers' lives. The solution to the problem of economic inequality cannot be that of educating workers out of factory jobs that would continue to exist. The goal should be to make those jobs more viable as sources of income.

---

[12] Rodriguez may not have declared himself to be on the left, but as Henry Staten argues, "Rodriguez's intense sense of class distinctions results in his arguably valid left critique of affirmative action." "Ethnic Authenticity, Class, and Autobiography: The Case of *Hunger of Memory*." (105). Staten, like *Race Class*, argues that because Rodriguez's analysis maintains class distinctions, Rodriguez can note how affirmative action benefits those already in a position to take advantage of the Ivy League.

Race Class thus analyzes texts published between 1981 and 1984, the era of neoliberalism's triumph, exemplified in such feats as Ronald Reagan's resounding defeat of the PATCO strike in 1981 and Margaret Thatcher's equally definitive defeat of the British miners' union in 1984. Finance was touted as beneficial for all classes (benefits that would eventually "trickle down") while workers' ability to collectively bargain for better wages, access to healthcare, and improved living conditions was actively stifled.[13] This understanding of the economy privileged a relatively unrestricted market and prevented market interventions in the form of labor protections. One need only look at the graphs tracking the rise of income inequality in the United States to see that the trickle did not occur.[14]

As neoliberalism flourished during the 1980s, the American university (which had steadily grown since the postwar boom of higher education) came to be understood as a mechanism enabling upward-class mobility. Having fostered the political unrest of the turbulent 1960s, the university also came to be seen as a preeminent site for the establishment of social justice. According to Chris Findeisen, the massive growth of American higher education "has fundamentally altered both its social function and its meaning within the cultural imagination" (286). Instead of being understood as a crucial mechanism producing and maintaining the class status quo (ever-increasing inequality enjoyed by the relative few), Findeisen argues that American institutions of higher education have come to be seen as a medium enabling social change, seemingly allowing access to the marginalized. Higher education became a gateway to a public sphere and republic of letters, now enhanced by a spirit of diversity and a welcoming sense of inclusion. Findeisen offers, as an example, Mark McGurl's optimistic historical narrative of the growth of creative writing programs, which McGurl presents in terms of a gradual inclusion of voices into the ambit of the university.

This view of the role of higher education, however, displaces the problem it claims to fix. "One of the greatest achievements of Mark McGurl's *The Program Era*, and of the novels it discusses," writes Findeisen, "has been to reinforce a vision of the university as a technology for increasing opportunity, democracy, and egalitarianism when [...] for most Americans the reality is quite different" (285). Citing staggering statistics, he shows how – despite increased access – the beneficiaries of higher education continue to be those of the higher classes.[15] The

---

[13] See Judith Stein's *The Pivotal Decade*.
[14] For just one example of such graphs, see Bui's "The Fall and Rise of U.S. Inequality, in 2 Graphs."
[15] Findeisen writes, "As for low-income students who overcome these obstacles and enroll in four-year universities – the vast expansion of the educational system has not improved their chances

postwar boom of higher education coincided with a severe increase in economic inequality, and the response to this increased inequality has been the hollow promise of upward-class mobility via a college education. This promise is made despite the fact that the fastest-growing and most available jobs are in retail, the service industry, and home healthcare and do not require a college degree at all. According to Walter Benn Michaels, "despite endless talk about the jobs of the future demanding a higher education, only five of [the fastest growing jobs] require a B.A. In other words, you'll need to have a college degree for about 7.25 million of these jobs; for the other 30 million, you don't" ("The Political Economy of Anti-Racism" 111). Not only do most of the fastest-growing jobs not require an undergraduate degree, but the jobs that do require it are "the high-paying ones. Which is the whole economic point of going to college and which is why higher education has nothing to do with equality" ("The Political Economy of Anti-Racism" 111). The promise that higher education makes to its students is that they will be the beneficiaries of inequality.

So, whereas Robbins and North present the university – particularly the study of literature – as enabling a progressive path toward a better society, Findeisen argues that the university and postwar literature have not only ensured the maintenance of severe class inequality but also legitimized this inequality's continued existence. Postwar American literature, specifically the "American campus novel," has helped "redescrib[e] the postwar university as an institution that can combat social inequality" by "making invisible a social inequality that the university not only doesn't combat but helps to legitimate" (285). How? The neoliberal view of higher education describes upward-class mobility as equally available to anyone who works hard enough to achieve it. But suppose that everyone can have access to a college education; suppose further that everyone has access even to the Ivy League. Not everyone will have access to the higher-paying jobs, which are far less available. As Findeisen argues, education cannot solve the problem of inequality because it offers a "supply-side approach to job creation" (295). Education focuses on improving "the quality of workers, not the quality of their jobs" (Findeisen 295). The far more available jobs would remain low-paying, poorly resourced, and unprotected. If the workers who gain

---

of success. Since 1970 educational opportunities for the least-advantaged students have stagnated. The chances of earning a bachelor's degree by age twenty-four have only improved for those who come from families in the upper half of the nation's income distribution (Sacks 118). For students coming from the poorest quartile, *the chances of graduating from college have scarcely risen above 6%, even as the chances for the children of the upper-middle quartile have almost doubled, from 14.9% in 1970 to 26.8% in 2002"* (130; original emphasis). For studies of Mexican American student enrollment in higher education, see *Advancing in Higher Education: A Portrait of Latina/o College Freshmen at Four-Year Institutions, 1975–2006*. See also Sylvia Hurtado, "Trend Analyses from 1971 to 2012 on Mexican American/Chicano Freshmen: Are We Making Progress?"

those jobs instead of the more lucrative ones are not disqualified because of discrimination, their resulting poverty will be considered unfortunate but not necessarily unjust. The resulting inequalities will be understood as inevitable when everyone has a fair shot at a meritocracy.

The question concerning the value of Mexican American literature was thus dramatized during a period when the needs of those left behind by the political economy were too often unarticulated. And the way this value was framed in the texts I study is, in a word, instructive. Of the responses to the question, Wherefore Mexican American literature? *Race Class* tracks what I characterize as two aesthetics that stem from two competing understandings of the nature of literary expression. One understands literature as an expression of one's identity, cultural ethnicity, and familial and ancestral ties. I place this aesthetic within McGurl's insightful account of the rise of "high cultural pluralism" (32) that has been a feature of the postwar boom of creative writing programs in higher education. High cultural pluralism, writes McGurl, merges "the high literary values of modernism," including the celebration of the individual artistic genius, "with a fascination with the experience of cultural difference and the authenticity of the ethnic voice" (32). McGurl describes how the writing workshop dictums of "write what you know" and "find your voice" establish the means to reconcile the individual with group cultural authenticity (23).

The other understanding of art, which we began to see in *Famous*, seeks to distance the reader from the depicted characters, disabling identification to thereby enable the reader's critical assessment. I place this aesthetic within a different modernist legacy, one exemplified in the writing of Bertolt Brecht. I return to Brecht in Sections 5 and 9, but for now, I invoke his distinction between "epic" and "dramatic" forms of theater to set the stage. For Brecht, "Epic theater" facilitates an audience's catharsis by soliciting its identification and sympathy, while "Dramatic theater" promotes dis-identification and evaluative distance (*Brecht* 37). The audience is not meant to sympathize with the characters so much as to understand the framing context of their situations. Stated with a degree of generality that the following will make concrete, the high cultural pluralism of what McGurl describes as the Program Era tends to foster an aesthetic of identification and sympathy instead of an aesthetic of estrangement and critique.

Without wanting to provide too prescriptive a taxonomy, I show how the aesthetics I track follow the basic outlines of the "redistribution or recognition" debate best exemplified by the philosophers Nancy Fraser and Alex Honneth.[16]

---

[16] Recognizing the increasing salience of demands for recognition, both Fraser and Honneth seek to understand the relationship between calls for the redistribution of resources and calls for the recognition and celebration of difference. Honneth insists that redistribution is nested within a more profound moral struggle for recognition embedded in the search for the good life (8).

I characterize the high cultural pluralism of McGurl's program era as "recognitional," and I characterize the Brechtian modernist aesthetic of estrangement as "redistributive." The recognitional aesthetic rejects calls for assimilation and emphasizes how literature enables a shared identity that demands to be recognized as distinct and valuable. The recognitional insists on recalling the past, remembering colonial violence monumentalized in ancestral ruins and graves. Recognitional literature often represents a unification with the past in scenes involving pilgrimages to these ruins, visits that bolster an identity shared by the writer and the people he or she represents. This strengthening of identity combats injustice by circulating the stories of the marginalized and oppressed. I describe this narrative circulation as the "testimonial function" of recognitional literature, which seeks to promote the stories of the silenced and ignored. As a witness offering the testimony of his or her people, the writer's identity matters and is emphasized to enhance the writer's ethos. By diversifying literary canons (through the preservation and circulation of a culture) and by representing the voice of the silenced (through the work's testimonial function), the recognitional seeks to provide a necessary path toward a more just world.

The redistributive aesthetic critiques this testimonial function of literature by emphasizing the rift between the writer and the people he or she is assumed to represent. It does so by highlighting the mechanisms of representation instead of seeking to circumvent them. The redistributive shows how the celebration of a shared culture occludes the fundamental class inequality that separates the writer and the poor. This competing aesthetic thus explicitly rejects scenes of ancestral unification via pilgrimages to ancient ruins. It averts identification (between reader and text, reader and writer) and questions the possibility of a shared, unchanging culture. The redistributive aesthetic shows how the preservation of culture not only does not address the structural economic problems but also worsens them by obstructing their causes. The point of literature, as demonstrated in this aesthetic, is not to testify nor to affirm an identity. Rather, the point is to discomfit readers' complacency and thereby, as Brecht would have it, prompt structural change.

Without understanding economic concerns within a moral framework, he argues, calls for redistribution will fail to address the more fundamental needs of love and belonging. Fraser concedes the importance of recognition but understands it as categorically distinct from the problem of class inequality. Fraser describes calls for recognition as participating in a broader "decoupling of cultural politics from social politics, of the politics of difference from the politics of equality" (8). Whereas the politics of difference rejects a universalist frame that appears to require assimilation, the politics of equality suggests that the reification of differences and the protection of distinctive cultures could disable cross-cultural solidarity. While both philosophers agree that the demands for recognition are crucial, they fundamentally disagree about the efficacy of these demands to produce structural change to benefit the poor and working classes.

The recognitional and the redistributive thus participate in a broader dialogue concerning whose voices are included in academia, whether symbolic inclusion addresses class inequalities, and whether literature, as such, is inevitably a tool, as Guillory describes, for "the reproduction of the social order" (*Cultural* ix). Could "subalterns" speak for themselves, or do they require organic intellectuals to function as mediators?[17] No longer able to presume their status as spokespersons, writers of the 1980s began to acknowledge how their class status – often the result of their college education – set them apart from the poor and working classes. To what extent *does* a culture unify disparate Mexican Americans into a community? Do Mexican American writers and artists represent this community's demands? Was the advancement of culture adequate for the task of garnering fairer wages for workers? Is the major problem Mexican Americans face that of *exclusion* from dominant mechanisms of wealth and social power (in which case, calls for inclusion and recognition point to a solution)? Or is the problem one of *exploitation* (in which case, inclusion into an exploitative system would not suffice)?

With such questions in the background, both the recognitional and redistributive fiction of the 1980s developed responses by featuring the "metafictional reflexivity" of "autopoiesis," McGurl describes.[18] In the novels I analyze, the narratological discourse self-consciously dramatizes the conditions that enable the narrative's coming into being. Each novel proleptically imagines the conditions enabling the emergence of the author figure, a temporal projection into the future that loops back to the narrative's beginning. This auto-narration produces the justification for the very existence of the novel by thematizing its need (why it emerged) and function (what work it will do). Although the Chicano novels of the 1970s sometimes featured a similar sense of auto-narration, wherein the Chicano writer emerges to coalesce a community's collective voice, the newer generation of novelists differs by highlighting the role of higher education in the development of the coalescing voice.[19] Islas' protagonist is a college professor

---

[17] In 1984, Gayatri Spivak highlighted this later question in an essay titled, "Can the Subaltern Speak?" in which she argued that academics' efforts to provide a voice to the marginalized compounds the very silence they seek to remedy. Spivak first delivered the essay at the 1983 conference, "Marxism and the Interpretation of Culture." For a reprint of the essay, see Nelson and Grossberg 271. For an example of the conservative backlash, see Dinesh D'Souza's *Illiberal Education*.

[18] The circular logic of "autopoiesis" McGurl analyzes employs the writing workshop platitudes: the writer's experience ("write what you know") informs and reflects the creative act of producing literature ("find your voice"), both of which are equally enabled and informed by the attention to craft, technique, and style featured so heavily in writing workshops ("show, don't tell"). This self-reflexive writing process fosters the "metafictional reflexivity" readers have come to associate with ambitious, self-consciously literary fiction that is simultaneously a product of creative writing programs and a metafictional critique of the imposing institutional procedures that would otherwise stifle individual creativity (McGurl 23).

[19] See Tomás Rivera's *... y no se lo trago la tierra* for an example of a novel that narrates the development of the Chicano writer who emerges to coalesce a community's voice.

who wonders if his acquired status separates him from his family. Cisneros' protagonist is a young girl who may be on the path to college so she can return to help those she leaves behind. James' protagonist may never go to college, but his school counselor insists that he develop his sense of ethnic self and try.

By tracking the development of the two aesthetics, *Race Class* offers a way of considering the history of American cultural production since the 1960s and the relation of this production to political debate. Through original readings of foundational Mexican American writers of the 1980s, I describe the Chicano origins of the recognitional aesthetic in Mexican American literature. I articulate why the redistributive aesthetic emerged as a critique and show how the aesthetic that gained the most traction within the context of higher education has been the recognitional, which has all but foreclosed the redistributive. Because literary critics and historians operate *within* the recognitional aesthetic, I argue, they misunderstand its politics and misinterpret its literature. As I demonstrate in what follows, critics can mischaracterize a critique of identity politics as "neoliberal" while claiming that celebrations of diversity and inclusion are inherently politically progressive. This misdiagnosis is the result of the predominance of the recognitional. The following pages explain why this predominance took place.

2 The Development of Chicano Literature and Culture

Chicano writers of the 1960s and 1970s raised the question of the function of literature, art, and culture with an urgency that responded to the existing narratives about Mexicans in literature, sociology, and anthropology. Mexicans had not been afforded the full spectrum of character development and expression in American literature.[20] In the social sciences, researchers characterized Mexican and Mexican American culture as creating unproductive values that precluded assimilation and participation in electoral politics. The culture was blamed for Mexican American poverty, high drop-out rates, and high instances of teenage pregnancy.[21] Popular texts, such as David Riesman, Reuel Denney, and Nathan Glazer's bestselling *The Lonely Crowd: A Study of the Changing American Character* (1950), described how "tradition-directed" parents (they explicitly mention Mexican parents) bestow suffocating traditions that negatively dictate individuals' choices and preclude productive assimilation practices. Oscar Lewis' *Five Families: Mexican Case Studies in the Culture of Poverty* (1959) argued that the compensatory set of values, beliefs, and practices developed among Mexico's poorest and most vulnerable

---

[20] See the anthology, *Chicano: From Caricature to Self-Portrait*, which includes stories by John Steinbeck, Jack London, and Bret Harte.

[21] For examples of this kind of research, from anthropology to sociology, see Edmonson, Heller, and Madsen. For an influential critique of these studies, see Romano-V 13–26.

populations comprised a "design for living," a "way of life" – in a word, a "culture" – that was passed down generationally along family lines. Lewis argued that even as the structural conditions change – through, say, upward-class mobility – the "culture of poverty" proves to be persistent.[22] In short, the observation that something was fundamentally wrong with Mexican Americans' behavior resulted in the conclusion that their culture was to blame.

During the mid-1960s, Mexican Americans circulated counter-narratives that celebrated Mexican American culture by proclaiming a proud, collective identity. The term *Chicano*, which had been used to convey negative connotations about poor migrant workers in the early 20th century, became a positive, intentional assertion of a collective sensibility based on a shared productive culture.[23] The efflorescence of Chicano literature of the second half of the twentieth century provided the artistic basis for consolidating the Chicano (today, more often called Chicanx) identity. Insofar as American literature and university research had produced the facile caricatures of Mexican American culture, Chicanos sought to change the narratives circulating within academia by providing the methodological and theoretical foundation of a people's existence, unity, and perseverance. Chicano literature worked alongside a newer Chicano-informed social science to produce the ground of an identity, and Chicanos created venues to publish their own work. They established the first Chicano-owned publisher, Quinto Sol Publications, in Berkeley, California, in 1967. Quinto Sol produced a quarterly journal, *El Grito: A Journal of Contemporary Mexican-American Thought*, that provided a forum for literary and visual works of art, as well as articles dismantling the social sciences' account of the inadequacies of Mexican culture. The journal, *Aztlan: Chicano Journal of the Social Sciences and the Arts*, established at UCLA in 1970, provided a forum for Chicano-informed social sciences and art. The first three articles in the inaugural 1970 issue of *Aztlan*, for example, offer an argument about the existence of such entities as "Mexican Americans," an argument for the existence of a distinctly Mexican American "culture," a culture that could provide the unity of a people.[24]

---

[22] See Lewis' *Five Families*. For a useful, condensed summary of his thesis, see Lewis' introduction to *La Vida*.

[23] According to Harth and Baldwin, "the term *Chicano* is, for the younger Mexican-American, more than simply a term for one's ethnic origin or cultural identity, as it stands also for an active political consciousness that will no longer tolerate second-class citizenship" (3). See also Gómez-Quiñones' description of how "wider public usage of the term as the self-designation for the community appeared in the sixties, when it was given political connotations by young activists" (*Chicano Politics* 7).

[24] The first three articles of this issue are Penalosa's "Toward an Operational Definition of the Mexican American," Hernández's "La Raza Satellite System," and Jaime Sena Rivera's "Chicanos."

While understanding the importance of building their own publishing venues, Chicanos also understood the college classroom – particularly the literature classroom – to be an important site of resistance and education. The study of Chicano literature could dispel the myths of cultural pathology. Richard Vasquez's novel, *Chicano* (1970), dramatizes this view of literature's capacity by depicting a college sociology classroom wherein a professor assigns his students a fieldwork assignment to determine why Mexican American students drop out of high school at higher rates. The professor warns the students, "If any of you reports back here that you've discovered the dropout problem is caused by the cultural barriers I'll personally brain you. We know all that. We want to know *what* in the cultural barrier is so insurmountable to the individual and *why*. It's complex" (287). The novel shows how the supposedly objective social scientist presupposes the problem to *be* cultural, leading his students to attend to their subjects with this methodological bias. *Chicano* thus highlights the difference between a supposedly detached academic knowledge and a more subjective lived experience when it points out how a white sociology graduate student in this class, David Stiver, "had relatively little contact with Spanish-speaking people, although he'd done a term paper on the plight of 750,000 Mexican-Americans in Texas" (289). David's limited academic knowledge lacks firsthand interactions with the people he claims to describe.

Vasquez's narrative strategy in *Chicano* presents the assumptions and stereotypes involving Mexican Americans and then shows the humanity that the stereotypes distort. When David finally goes to the home of his assigned research subjects, he rests on his assumptions, mistakenly thinking that the matriarch will offer him chocolate and tortillas. He later notices "an ancient cowhide" hanging in their home, for which he "tried to compose a likely history for the hide, but could not" (308). What he cannot do – construct an explanatory story – the novel can: The first half of the novel had already provided the cowhide's history. The novel thus demonstrates the value of literature about Mexican Americans, which can help expose false narratives by providing rich stories of peoples' lives.

Although it exposes the shortcomings of false assumptions, the novel does not explicitly highlight the strength of a culture that could productively unite disparate Mexican and Mexican Americans. In the novel's plot, David begins to date his research subject, named Marianna, who takes him to her Mexican grandparents' home (in which the grandmother *does* offer him chocolate and tortillas). He notes how something had changed in the transition from her grandparents' Mexican traditions to Marianna's Mexican American way of life. He judges her as having "no sophistication [...] Actually, he saw, she had no culture. Her home, her parents, were barren of culture in the national sense. The family pattern of tradition, the language, everything about her was composite. If there was a culture here, it was the culture of being a subculture. Hers was not the culture of poverty as he had studied poverty" (304). Although the novel appears to expose the shortcomings of the culture of poverty thesis, through this white sociology student's perspective, the novel also appears to acknowledge a supposed cultural void in the "composite" Mexican American way of life. The novel's tragic conclusion (involving pregnancy, drugs, and dropping out of school) appears to affirm the stereotypical view of cultural pathology after all.

Vasquez's contemporaries criticized his novel for inadequately representing a people and for apparently confirming the social sciences' negative view. According to the Chicano novelist Tomás Rivera, Vasquez had produced a mere "reflection of a false interpretation of the Chicano, sociologically and anthropologically" ("Labyrinth" 266). Rivera's friend and fellow Chicano novelist Rolando Hinojosa agrees when he writes that Vasquez's *Chicano*, "to a considerable degree, has served as a misleading sociological interpretation of the Chicano" ("Toward" 10). Rivera and Hinojosa's novels instead represent the disparate voices of multiple characters inextricably linked to their community. Rivera's *... y no se lo tragó la tierra* (1971), which won the first Quinto Sol literary prize, offers a collection of vignettes that tell the story of a young boy who will come to recognize his relationships with those around him. The boy emerges as an author figure who will coalesce the voices he hears within his community. Hinojosa's English version of his novel, *Estampas del valle* (1973), which won the third Quinto Sol literary prize, begins with a prefatory note that describes the writer's role as being that of a "compiler" (xiv). Hinojosa's novel, according to the note, is not a "figment of someone's imagination" but is instead the compilation of recorded voices and incidents (xiv). Both Rivera and Hinojosa's novels dramatize the rise of the Chicano literary artist who becomes a conduit for the voice of the people.

The value of reading a distinctly Chicano literature centers on its ability to foreground a proud sense of community. Chicano-informed social sciences, literature, and art produced the ground for an identity, uniting Mexican Americans with a shared sense of culture meant to embody their interests. While Mexican and Mexican American culture was deemed to be the problem by midcentury social scientists, Chicanos demonstrated culture as the solution.

3 The Limits of the Chicano Solution

This characterization of the problem *as* cultural, however, risked ensuring that a politics of recognition would be pursued at the expense of a politics of redistribution. In 1977, Chicano historian Juan Gómez-Quiñones recognized the tendency of cultural appreciation to supplant material efforts to address workers' needs. In an essay titled "Toward a Concept of Culture," he shows how the ethnic Mexican American culture that came to take the name, *Chicano*, is not synonymous with a working-class politics. "The problem of culture," writes Gómez-Quiñones, "consists of understanding its makeup and its process historically and in contemporary times and understanding the relation of culture to conflict both conceptually and politically" (29). By "understanding culture historically," Gómez-Quiñones means understanding it dialectically in relation to the structural conditions that enable its emergence. Such a culture, he argues, must actively be placed in the service of the specific class struggle of its time by academics who, operating as organic intellectuals, continually foreground class as the problem to be solved.[25] Without this sustained effort that connects culture to a class politics, culture will remain complicit in class inequality. "In sum," he writes, "this essay explores the 'problemática de ser Mexicanos y trabajadores' [the problematic of being Mexicans and workers]. The task is to work to bring about cultural unity on a given basis to a given end" (29). Gómez-Quiñones, in short, does not take as a given the conflation of the terms Chicanos and workers. Without a conscious effort by organic leaders, "culture" could not serve as the glue holding together their interests.

The question that Gómez-Quiñones leaves unaddressed, however, is whether the term *Chicano* could provide the interclass solidarity he advocates. Historically, that has not been the case because the "given end" to which Chicano culture has continually been brought to bear has been the perpetuation of the ethnic identity the culture helps enable. Without the attention that places cultural intervention in the service of a working-class agenda, Chicano nationalism diverges from working-class politics.

We need only to read the first-hand accounts of the student organizers involved in the Chicano Movement to see the conceptual roots of this divergence. According to Carlos Muñoz, one of the organizers of the 1968 high school student walkouts and president of the student organization UMAS (United Mexican American Students), the normative framework for understanding the Chicano Movement as such is a "politics of identity or the identity problematic" (Muñoz 19). Muñoz makes it clear that the identity problematic (what I am calling the "recognitional") operates *alongside* the working-class political struggles affecting Mexican Americans, yet their goals are not

---

[25] The term *organic intellectual*, developed by Antonio Gramsci, helps describe the relationship between this work and that of other strata of a collective that took the name, "Chicano community." Antonio Gramsci theorized the concept of the organic intellectual in the notes published as *Selections from the Prison Notebooks of Antonio Gramsci*. See Gramsci's "The Intellectuals" 49–57.

homologous. The conflation of labor organizing with identity politics, he argues, has led to the *mischaracterization* of César Chávez as a leader of the Chicano Movement. "The farmworker struggle led by César Chávez has been the most glaring example of misinterpretation," he writes, because "Chávez was the leader of a labor movement and later a union struggle *that was never an integral part of the Chicano Movement*" (19; emphasis added). According to Muñoz, Chávez "made it clear, especially during the movement's formative years, that the farmworkers' union did not support Chicano nationalism or neo-separatism" because he was an "organizer of a union representing a multiracial constituency of rank-and-file workers" (19). This working-class insistence on foregrounding the solidarity based on workers' rights was fundamentally *different* from what Muñoz describes as the Chicano "quest for a new identity and for political power" and "Chicano self-determination" (26). Chicanos strived for the development of "*La Nueva Raza*, a new people proud of their Mexican working-class culture" (26). Working-class culture, in Muñoz's view, is something to be maintained and respected. The "leaders of working-class organizations," though, "have largely forsaken the question of ethnic identity and promoted the class interests of the workers in the organization of strikes and unions" (20). Insofar as there was an overlap between the working class and "Chicanos," the status of being "working-class" in Muñoz's characterization appears as something like a badge of honor one would not want to trade in, a "culture" one would not want to change.

Muñoz's argument that Chávez was not a Chicano leader might be surprising, yet his emphasis on Chicano nationalism and ethnicity is entirely in accord with the conceptual basis of the Chicano identity. In the second article published in the journal *Aztlan* in 1970, sociologist Deluvina Hernández specifies the very foundation of Chicano unity: the concept of *La Raza* (The Race). As the Chicano unifying principle, "La Raza" is categorically different from the working class:

> The Mexican American, although included in the proletariat, is not an oppressed class, per se. It is instead an oppressed ethnic group. Thus identified, the Mexican American ethnic group will not readily seek to abolish itself in order to abolish the oppressive conditions, as Marx would have the oppressed classes do. The reverse is in fact the case: Mexican Americans seek to maintain their identity while abolishing the oppressive conditions, utilizing the concept of nationalism as the ideological framework for community organizing. (29)

The evident overlap between working-class concerns and Chicanismo appeared to suggest a homologous entity (Muñoz's "Mexican working-class culture"). Yet the fundamental difference between Chicano nationalism (based on the concept of *La Raza*) and working-class political activism (evident in union organizing) points to a divergence in conceptual *framing* and goals. In her essay, Hernández hails an ethnic community into being by identifying its unifying principle (*La Raza*) and places a burden of responsibility on that community's educated class. She writes, as "college students entered the cultural, educational, economic and political arena," they did so "on behalf of 'La Raza'" (29). With this conceptual framing, such college students could see themselves as representing the lives of their community, advancing their needs by voicing their interests. As José F. Aranda explains, Hernández's argument sought to "consolidate a larger nonacademic political identity, while also promoting university leadership of that constituency, a blueprint for future organizing and for the movement vanguard" (15). Yet, he argues, "The middle and upper classes of any ethnic group historically have been adverse to collective action in the United States, except where ethnicity is the primary basis for political action; the Mexican American community proved no different" (15–16). So, despite the arguments for an organic form of college leadership that remained attuned to the needs of the working class, the fight to preserve an ethnic culture could proceed independently of the fight to address economic exploitation.

We can again see this divergence enacted in the career of Luis Valdez, whose *Teatro Campesino* helped César Chávez encourage union organizing by celebrating a shared culture. Valdez's play, *Los Vendidos* (meaning both "the sold ones" and "the sellouts"), for example, depicts the necessity of college-educated Chicanos to remain faithful to their community by using their collective voice to advocate for the needs of the poor. In the play, the exclamations, "¡Viva la raza!" and "¡Viva la huelga!" ("Long live the race!" and "Long live the strike!") appear as mutually supportive slogans, again emphasizing the significant overlap of the Chicano Movement and labor organizing (51). Yet, according to Muñoz, Valdez wanted "to locate the union in the framework of a Chicano nationalist ideology" while Chávez did not. Valdez and the Teatro Campesino thus left Chávez's labor movement "precisely because Chávez did not agree with Valdez's efforts" (Muñoz 17). Valdez went on to receive acclaim on Broadway and Hollywood with his popular play *Zoot Suit* (1978; adapted to film in 1981) and the film *La Bamba* (1987). Valdez did not become a "vendido" because he maintained his focus on the Chicano identity and provided Broadway and Hollywood audiences with the thematic content to feel connected to a Chicano sense of self. This effort, though, could and did proceed independently of a labor movement that necessitated union organization and cross-cultural, cross-ethnic solidarity.

This divergence between a recognitional identity and redistributive class politics is present even in César Chávez's explicitly working-class political intervention. As a union organizer, Chávez used Chicano iconography to promote solidarity. Chávez and Dolores Huerta's National Farm Workers Association helped organize a grape strike in Delano, California, responding to, as Yolanda Broyles-González catalogs, the "exploitation by growers, crew leaders, and parasitic labor contractors; the widespread use of child labor; pesticide and herbicide poisoning; substandard housing; generally inhumane working and living conditions; and no health or other benefits" (xi). Graphic posters called for solidarity during these labor strikes and product boycotts.[26] According to historian Jefferson Cowie, however, Chávez embodies "irreconcilable values" spiritually held in the "twin souls of Chavez's life – spiritual/civil rights leader and labor leader" (54). According to Cowie, "the patron saint of *Chicanismo* continued to live on, bolstering the civil rights of Mexican Americans [...] but the union cause died out" (54). Chávez's charisma, which galvanized sociocultural fervor, did not operate as effectively in the more mundane, day-to-day world of labor organizing. Cowie acknowledges the difficulty and courage involved in consolidating a distinctly Mexican American identity; yet, he argues that this identity "fused more easily with American political traditions of individual civil rights than did the unionization of the farmworkers for collective economic rights and the material betterment of those who toiled in the fields" (49–54). Extrapolating from Cowie's analysis, one can see how the Chicano intervention was ultimately not a critique of market exploitation so much as an argument against the exploitation of certain types of bodies with certain histories. Stated differently, the Chicano intervention attempted to ensure that Chicanos were no longer sorted into exploitative labor pools, becoming instead the market's beneficiaries.

Such a divergence between the tactics seeking to enable ethnic recognition and preservation, on one hand, and the organizing efforts seeking to secure rights for workers and the poor, on the other, recurs throughout the history of the Chicano Movement. Seeking to correct biased exclusion, those pursuing a politics of recognition appear to accept the basic outlines of a society's structural formation. They seek the equality of opportunity to join its ranks as the beneficiaries. As literary scholar Marcial González puts it, "The former [identity politics] is premised upon experience, while the latter [class politics] is premised upon class as structure" (35). This difference, he argues, explains why identity "group formations promote strategies for unity directed at correcting democratic inequalities – broadening the possibilities for civic inclusion and participation – which are worthy causes in and of themselves, but which are not aimed at comprehending, much less eliminating, the systemic causes of

---

[26] See Carmen's *¡Printing the Revolution!*

inequality" (35). González thus repeats the conclusion reached by Deluvina Hernández, that the "working class" and "the Chicano" are separate categories. He reiterates "the problem" identified by Gómez-Quiñones in 1977 – the "problem of culture" that ensues when one considers "the problem of being Mexicans *and* workers" (Gómez-Quiñones 29).

Cowie and González remain sympathetic to the efforts of Chicano activism. Yet, they both identify a trend: Upper classes tend to agree on cultural issues at the exclusion of addressing the issues of class inequality. As González argues, "Political practices aimed at challenging oppression are important and absolutely necessary, but without a class standpoint they nonetheless remain contained within an ideology of systemic maintenance and reform, despite the many admirable, courageous, and even sometimes life-threatening actions carried out against the various forms of social abuse and injustice" (35). By identifying the need for a sustained "class standpoint," González repeats Gómez-Quiñones' call to organic intellectuals to continually place culture in the service of a class politics. González, however, makes a much stronger claim about organic intellectuals committed to ethnic unity: Insofar as upper classes tend to organize around cultural issues, they tend to occlude the problem of class. He writes, "group identities are more likely to obfuscate or mystify the same relations, especially with regard to social class, than to encourage revolutionary change to take place" (35).

Because of the exigencies of the oppressive discriminatory atmosphere they faced, young Chicano activists – operating under the banner of *La Raza* and framing their struggles as a politics of identity – appear to have pushed for a strategic, unified front that, in effect, downplayed class inequality while claiming to address it. In *Chicano Politics*, Gómez-Quiñones describes how the student arm of the Chicano Movement, including the groups MAYO and MEChA (El Movimiento Estudiantil Chicano de Aztlan), eventually disbanded because of "a loss of organizational direction and purpose, ironically caused by an inability to develop viable goals after achieving initial success in increasing the numbers of Mexican students and establishing Chicano studies programs" (119). Interclass solidarity had to be established and maintained over time. That this effort to sustain a class focus proved untenable suggests that "the problem of culture" did not provide the solidarity focusing on the problems of class.

Indeed, if, in "Toward a Concept of Culture" in 1977, Gómez-Quiñones was still hopeful about organic intellectuals' ability to use culture as a means toward class solidarity, by 2014, he came to see 1977 as the very year the Chicano Movement lost its momentum because of a dispersed focus (Gómez-Quiñones and Vásquez). In *Making Aztlán: Ideology and Culture of the Chicano*

Movement (2014), Gómez-Quiñones and coauthor Irene Vásquez argue that by 1977, "previous tenuous camaraderies faded as did an ethos-driven will to act in concert" (6). Citing a well-attended Immigrant Rights Conference held in San Antonio, Texas, Gómez-Quiñones and Vásquez highlight the conference's "transnational ethos," which they read as indicative of the dissolution of Chicano as a unifying term that could address specific, targeted goals (6). Organic intellectuals failed to maintain a class focus when the unifying principle was ethnic culture. Their activism ultimately treated the problem of recognition as a proxy for the problem of redistribution, risking leaving the latter unaddressed.

4 A Critique of Chicano Activism and Literature: Richard Rodriguez *Hunger of Memory* (1982)

By the 1980s, the ideal of the Chicano organic intellectual, someone who would explicitly connect an ethnic culture to a class politics, had reached a point of crisis. No other writer of this era applied as much pressure to Chicano activism as Richard Rodriguez. His infamous collection of autobiographical essays, *Hunger of Memory* (1982), articulated a trenchant challenge. Rodriguez confronted some of the Chicanos' most firmly held beliefs: namely, that Chicano literature helped to produce the ground for class solidarity and efforts to increase Chicano representation in college (in the undergraduate population, on the faculty, and in the curriculum) would lead to a progressive political future that would help the poor and working classes.

The activism that focused on increasing the number of Mexican Americans in higher education was limited because it ignored crucial features that contributed to their lower representation – namely, their inability to afford tuition and the gross disparities in their education that precluded them from even applying. Rodriguez thus questions the pervasive valorization of the college campus as the site enabling upward-class mobility because those already in a position to avail themselves of elite opportunities (including college enrollment and eventual professorships) are, strictly speaking, not the most vulnerable members of society. "The campus," he argues, "has become a place for 'making it' rather than a place for those who, relatively speaking, already 'have it made'" (165). Those with the preparation to be accepted into higher education, especially more elite institutions, have already benefitted from their access to college preparatory classes, exposure to literacy and tutoring services, and more effective forms of education by virtue of their family's private funding or higher-income neighborhoods' public schooling.

Rodriguez's insistence on the importance of class renders his critique of affirmative action a "left critique" even if he does not speak from the position of the left (Staten, 105). "Remarkably, affirmative action passed as a program of the Left," he writes, a fact that is "remarkable" because it "disregard[ed] the importance of class" and "assum[ed] that the disadvantages of the lower class would necessarily be ameliorated by the creation of an elite society" (145–6). By focusing on race-based initiatives to increase the number of Mexican Americans at universities, activists effectively advance a political agenda disproportionately benefiting the children of the middle and upper-middle classes. Low-wage manual laborers were left to fend for themselves while being rhetorically included in a supposed Chicano cultural unity. Rodriguez instead insists that the term Chicano be dismantled to expose the class distinctions it occludes. Rodriguez's analysis insists on maintaining one's view on class distinctions to thereby assess what efforts benefit the poor and working classes and which do not.

The columnist Rubén Navarrette affirms Rodriguez's argument when describing the demanding standards required for entry into the Ivy League. Navarrette describes his first days at Harvard as a college freshman in 1985, "Of the entering class of just over 1,600 freshmen, I was one of only 35 Mexican-Americans" (56). Apart from the low number of Mexican American first-year students, "it was impossible not to notice the 'quality' of those who had made it through Harvard's half-opened door" (56). "We had been carefully chosen it seemed," he writes, "We were valedictorians, star athletes, class presidents, and National Merit Scholars. We were, in short, the crema of the Mexican crop" (56). Rodriguez calls this cream ("crema") of the crop the "elite society," those fortunate enough to avail themselves of the opportunities for upward-class mobility (145).

Mexican Americans, though, have always trailed behind their "white" counterparts in terms of family income. Studying the trends of first-year students from 1975 to 2006, Sylvia Hurtado et al. show how "in dollar terms, the household income gap between Latina/os and non-Hispanic White Students has grown" since 1975 to a "*fourfold increase*" by 2006 (*Advancing in Higher Education* 10). What has come to be called the "racial wealth gap" appears to expose Rodriguez's characterization of a Chicano "elite society" as misleading. Chicanos are disproportionately impoverished when compared to their white counterparts, a disparity that has only drastically increased. And yet, the term "Chicano" nominally erases the class distinctions *within* the category, and this erasure threatens to occlude the ways in which the top 10 percent of Chicanos will be more likely to benefit from higher education. When the group "Chicanos" as a whole is compared to the group "whites" as a whole, the largest disparity will be visible between the top 10 percent of each category. Studying the racial wealth gap between "white" and "black" households, Matt Bruening shows how "nearly all white wealth is owned by the top 10 percent of white households just as nearly all black wealth is owned by the top 10 percent of black households. The lower and middle deciles of each racial group own virtually none of their racial group's wealth." "What this means," argues Bruening, "is that the overall racial wealth disparity is being driven almost entirely by the disparity between the wealthiest 10 percent of white people and the wealthiest 10 percent of black people." Although the disparity between the races is evident throughout every class level in both groups, eliminating the racial gap would primarily benefit the top 10 percent of each race. Why? According to Bruening, closing the racial wealth gap would mean "redistributing a lot of wealth between the white and black upper classes. That's where the wealth is, and so that's where the wealth gap is." The real gap exists between the rich and poor, a gap that persists *within* racial groups. Closing the racial wealth gap would help those at the top 10 percent, but would leave the problem of economic inequality fundamentally unaddressed.

Connecting Bruening's analysis to Rodriguez's argument, we could begin to understand why the advancement of higher education benefits the upper classes while ignoring the problem of economic inequality. Even if the number of Chicano students admitted into college were to increase, students who have had access to these advantages will outperform those who have not. This problem will be exacerbated in the Ivy League, the demanding requirements of which will drastically narrow the pool of viable applicants. "Latina/os have made strides in recent years in terms of entrance to college in increasing numbers," write Hurtado et al., "However, access for Latina/o students is immaterial if not accompanied by adequate academic preparation prior to arriving in college" (*Advancing in Higher Education,* 11). Family income can increase access to resources, enabling academic preparation. So, although higher education is touted as the mechanism enabling upward social mobility and, therefore, a vehicle for the lower classes to improve their economic status, it tends to benefit those already in a position to avail themselves of the opportunity.

The dramatic increase in economic inequality, which has been evident since 1975, is visible in the median household income of first-year students at four-year colleges and universities. Hurtado et al. highlight how the "data show that parental income for entering freshmen at four-year colleges and universities has markedly increased as measured by students' reported median household income" (*Advancing in Higher Education* 9*)*. The family income of college applicants keeps increasing, but so does the economic gap between the rich and poor. The focus on closing the *racial* income gap ensures that the wealthiest Chicanos will match the wealthiest "white" families, yet the poor will not benefit from this wealth. And the focus on higher education assumes that the benefits will trickle down to the poor.

Writing in the wake of the Bakke decision, Rodriguez must have known the nail-against-the-chalkboard effect his position would elicit among his academic reading public, those for whom the university was understood as enabling justice by becoming a potential social equalizer. Rodriguez's historical account helps explain how, during the 1980s, anti-discrimination activism came to bracket a focus on class inequality. "Racism," Rodriguez argues, "rhetorically replaced poverty as the key social oppression" (160). Anti-racism, in turn, became a synecdoche for a progressive politics that could address inequality. Stated differently, a politics of recognition could replace a politics of redistribution and not be seen *as* a replacement.

Rodriguez's critique of Chicano identity politics identifies an ahistorical analogy between the African American and Mexican American collective experiences of discrimination. The specificity of legalized segregation created the conditions for a black, interclass political vision because Jim Crow laws did not differentiate between the "black businessman and the black maid" (160). "Thus," argues Rodriguez, "when segregation laws were challenged and finally defeated, the benefit to one became the benefit for all; the integration of an institution by a single black implied an advance for the entire race" (160). Because of the analogy between African and Mexican Americans, the institutional integration of Chicano scholars could similarly be characterized as an advancement for "the race."

Rodriguez contextualizes the emergence of Chicano activism by connecting it to the political fervor of other civil rights movements, the "liberation movements of women, the elderly, the physically disabled, and the homosexual" (160). He distinguishes this advocacy for civil rights from activism that focused explicitly on class inequality. The "lesson that survived the turbulence in the South of the fifties and sixties," he describes, was "that there are forms of oppression that touch all levels of a society" (160). Just as legal segregation did not discriminate in terms of class, misogyny and sexism affects *all* women. Activists against sexism, heterosexism, ageism, and ableism could thereby speak for all potential victims, regardless of their class position. This focus on the forms of discrimination that could affect anyone drew attention away from the specific issues of exploitation that specifically affected the poor and working classes. Thus, while undoubtedly legitimate, argues Rodriguez, "the woman business executive's claim to be the victim of social oppression" risks the danger of "ignor[ing] altogether the importance of *class*" (160 original emphasis). Similarly, although Rodriguez believes the "black lawyer" when the lawyer describes how "there is never a day in his life when he forgets he is black," Rodriguez reiterates the difference between the experiences of those in the upper-middle class who face discrimination and the lives of the working class structured by economic exploitation (161). His argument here is not that the women executive's and black lawyer's complaints are not worthy of redress, nor that misogyny and racism have not historically functioned to maintain the elite's privilege. Rather, the point is that efforts to diversify and adequately respect the elite – as he puts it, efforts to "form a leadership class" (145) – do not constitute a left politics. Such efforts are, in fact, antithetical to the definition of the left, for which the very caretaking of a "leadership class" constitutes a problem.

One of Rodriguez's central arguments, then, highlights the distinction between the privileged and the exploited, a difference that enables the former to declare their ways of life as expressions of their cultural identity. He describes how some of the migrant workers he would see in California wore "Texas *sombreros* and T-shirts which shone fluorescent in the twilight" (122), attire that contrasts with the "dandyism" of his own "double-breasted Italian suits and custom-made English shoes" (146). Stated simply, those who choose to wear fluorescent T-shirts and sombreros over tailored suits and bespoke shoes must have the means to make that choice. Those who select wide-brimmed hats and thin, sun-reflecting T-shirts to express their cultural preference – and not because they work in the sun all day – are manifesting a choice not everybody has. This is the reason why Rodriguez lambasts Mexican American college professors and undergrads for wearing the "costumes of the rural poor" (168): for them, the clothing functions as a sign of allegiance to a culture that eliminates class difference. When detached from the specific context that led to their use, articles of clothing become fashion statements. For Rodriguez, class privilege provides the luxury to enjoy as culture what for others amounts to necessities for survival.

He dramatizes how class privilege enables ethnic pride when describing an anguished encounter he experienced as a college student while working a summer job at a construction site. Rodriguez had taken the job out of a desire to connect with workers and to display what his mother always advised him to protect against the sun: his "dark skin." "Dark skin was for my mother the most important symbol of a life of oppressive labor and poverty" (127), he writes, exemplifying the text's intentionally naive conflation of terms denoting class (including *braceros*) and terms describing physical appearance (dark skin). *Braceros*, "those who work [outdoors] with their *brazos*, their arms [. . .] for very little money" (121), of course, had dark, sunburnt skin, yet Rodriguez comes to "envy [...] their physical lives, their freedom to violate the taboo of the sun" by sometimes working shirtless (135). Their indifference to the sun marked their unconsciousness of their skin. Stated differently, their indifference to their skin made them unconscious of its darkening. Upon arriving at his first construction site gig, "[n]o longer afraid," he takes off his shirt and "[a]t last become[s] like a *bracero*" (140–141). Just as shame might have been irrelevant to the shirtless workers, pride might also have been beside the point; yet, here, Rodriguez converts what amounts to a matter of indifference but obvious inconvenience into an exercise in self-esteem. Job-related side effects (being hot, getting burned by the sun) become the means for his self-acceptance.

At the job, however, Rodriguez encounters a group of "Mexican aliens," six men, whose ages ranged from twenty to sixty, hired for the day by a contractor to perform manual labor (144). Rodriguez calls them "[a]nonymous men" because the contractor never introduces them to the other workers, a separation he has the opportunity to bridge when asked by the contractor to convey a message to them in Spanish. Rodriguez imagines "engag[ing] them in small talk," thereby assuring himself of their shared "familiarity," yet agonizes about how to gain their trust (145). He considers asking them what part of Mexico they are from and, if necessary, lying to them that his parents were from there too. Ultimately, however, he finds himself simply relaying the message and saying nothing else. The familiarity that he fails to establish on ethnic grounds (their shared language and cultural heritage) appears to be made available momentarily by the seeming class solidarity of one man's response; he nonverbally acknowledges Rodriguez, then looks past him "toward *el patrón*." "For a moment," Rodriguez describes, "I felt swept up by that glance in the Mexicans' company" (145). Of course, Rodriguez may not be "*el patrón*," yet he is certainly not one of "*los pobres*" – his mother's term for those whom Marx would call the "surplus population."[27] His position, although also temporary and paid, is practically voluntary as he takes the summer job while enrolled at Stanford, "the school rich people went to" (139–140). At summer's end, he could and would leave the working poor and rejoin the university's rich.

The pivot on which his narrative turns – what separates the naive boy who conflates race with class from the man who writes the autobiography – is his realization of the limits of cultural identity because of his recognition of class inequality. His experience as a temporary worker offers this lesson because it highlights the fundamental difference between himself and "those who work

---

[27] For a useful account of the problematic usage of the term "surplus population [...] in all its declensions (the unemployed, the impoverished, immigrants, the excluded, the underclass, the insecurely employed, etc.)," see Zamora's "When Exclusion Replaces Exploitation."

with their bodies all their lives" (142). He was naively surprised that construction workers were diverse "middle-class Americans" whose interests could include Rothko's paintings. Yet, he comes to realize the disparity between the full-time construction workers, himself, and, most radically, the "*pobres*," the "anonymous men," the exploited undocumented workers. Try as he might to feel like he belonged, his very ability to luxuriate in the daily soreness of his muscles marked his status as a labor tourist, enjoying the workout. It is this acknowledgment of inequality – his awareness of the disparity between their class positions – that ultimately stops him from attempting to establish what he realizes will only be a facile sense of camaraderie with the Mexican workers. They, unlike his coworkers, are not even in the middle class.

This recognition of their unavailability to him is a function not of Rodriguez's personal relation to the men but, rather, the structural difference between them. Insofar as they are objectified, it is a result of capitalism and not his condescension. Their silence is thus an emblem of this objectification and structural division, a silence that ultimately haunts Rodriguez as he recalls their encounter. "Their silence is more telling" of their "disadvantaged condition," he writes. "They lack a public identity. They remain profoundly alien" (149). Thus, he argues that by advocating for cultural recognition rather than highlighting class inequality, "the middle class blurs the distinction so crucial to social reform" (5). By representing the culture of undocumented workers instead of foregrounding their "disadvantage," writers highlight their self-pride instead of arguing for the grounds enabling redress. For Rodriguez, they are, crucially, "Persons apart. People lacking a union obviously, people without grounds" (149), redress then taking the form of efforts to ensure job security, safe working conditions, living wages, health care, and legal protection against labor abuse.

It would not be an exaggeration to say that for almost forty years, the negative reaction against *Hunger of Memory* focuses, in part, on Rodriguez's refusal to give others a voice by representing the voice they already have. Tomás Rivera, writing in 1984, criticizes Rodriguez because he "offers no recognition of the cultural uniqueness of his parents" ("Hunger" 342). In 2015, John Alba Cutler repeats this criticism, arguing that Rodriguez's parents "appear silent only because Rodriguez fails to give them a voice" (95). Yet Rodriguez himself insists, "I do not give voice to my parents by writing about their lives. I distinguish myself from them by writing about the life we once shared" (202). His access to a privileged education does "distinguish" him from his parents (by allowing him to write the way he does and publish where he does) and *further* differentiates him from undocumented Mexican workers. This fundamental difference is not mitigated by whatever affective relation he might express towards either.

It is especially revealing, then, that Rodriguez did not write a novel. He contextualizes the emergence of ethnic literature within a broader literary history that links "the relationship of the novel to the rise of the middle class in eighteenth-century Europe" (173). By mentioning this coterminous development between a genre and a class, he means to prompt his readers to consider the class of the college-educated novelists privileged to write and the reading publics who have the leisure required to read. He considers Chicano literature as the literature produced by the middle class, enabling that class to appreciate and celebrate a cultural identity while professing to represent and circulate the voices of the exploited. By claiming to share a culture that unites their interests, the middle class tends to focus on ethnic issues of recognition – the representation, inclusion, and celebration of voices – which occludes the problems of redistribution. The cultural valuation of the poor's marginalized voices misunderstands what the poor as such need.

Rodriguez's autobiography thus distances itself from what he characterizes as a "new genre, 'ethnic literature'" (6). He dramatizes this rejection of the politics of ethnic literary representation by describing another agonized encounter, one that took place in his campus office during the late 1970s. A "group of eight or ten Hispanic students" approached him "to teach a 'minority literature' course at some barrio community center" because "[t]hey were certain that this new literature had an important role to play in helping to shape the consciousness of a people lacking adequate literary representation" (173). This confrontation could be understood as potentially compensating for the confrontation described previously: The precarious "anonymous men" described by Rodriguez *can* have a "public identity" and a "voice" because a literature provides it. But just as he had the opportunity to connect with Mexican workers but seemingly could not, in this encounter, Rodriguez has the opportunity to establish solidarity with the "Hispanic students" but will not. He highlights the futility of their efforts by arguing that writers do not represent the voices of the lower classes. "Any novel or play about the lower class will necessarily be alien to the culture it portrays," he argues, offering Alex Haley's *Roots* (1976) as a case in point. Haley's novel "tells us more about his difference from his illiterate, tribal ancestors than it does about his link to them" (173). Rodriguez's claim here is that novels, historically connected to the middle class, are inadequate vehicles to articulate the needs of the poor. From this perspective, Chicano literature amounts to a decidedly middle-class phenomenon, one that claims that the beneficiaries of upward-class mobility remain "unchanged" from their working-class "community" and thus share and advance their political interests (171).

Rodriguez's blunt characterization of Haley's ancestors as "illiterate" could strike readers as insensitive because he appears to use a Western measure of value (literacy) to judge people from the past, thereby ignoring their cultural contributions because they are not worthy of esteem. For Haley, however, *Roots* offers a different account than that of Western literacy. *Roots* exists within a continuum that connects Haley to his ancestors whose names the novel recites, thereby vivifying history and connecting the past to the present.[28] *Roots* dramatizes the testimonial function in its very opening scene, with Kunta Kinte's naming ceremony involving the gathering of the village and a recital of his forefathers' names, "which were great and many, [and] went back more than two hundred rains" (3). Echoes of this naming ritual resound towards the novel's conclusion, wherein Kinte's great-great-granddaughter, Cynthia, gathers a "houseful of family" and recites to her newborn daughter (Alex Haley's mother) "the whole story back to the African, Kunta Kinte" (659). Throughout the novel, Kinte's lineage maintains the oral tradition practiced by the African *griots*, "men who were in effect living, walking archives of oral history" (674). The novel, *Roots*, thus functions as an act of testimony and preservation, reinforcing the role of the African oral historians' task by assuming their place.

Rodriguez thus intentionally invokes the extremely popular *Roots*, the television adaptation of which topped the lists of most-watched television series, to highlight his rejection of recognitional literature and the recognitional politics it enables. In a preface to *Roots*, the sociologist Michael Eric Dyson credits the novel with inciting a national discourse about the continued relevance of slavery in American society. The novel, according to Dyson, provides a diagnosis of what constitutes American social injustice – "racial amnesia" (x) – and it prescribes a solution – "grappl[ing] with the past" (x). By reminding the nation of its sullied past and by reconnecting African Americans to their history, Dyson argues, *Roots* helps the country through "the long midnight of slavery's haunting presence" (xi). Dyson thus articulates a strong case for the politics of recognition that is enabled by recognitional literature's testimonial function tied to a notion of history that is embodied in the present not simply as a narrative of causality but as a spectral haunting attached to bodies of the oppressed.

---

[28] Haley describes how the death of the African *griots* constitutes the loss of a living library, the potential erasure of which entails the eradication of present-day identities: "The memories and the mouths of ancient elders was the only way that early histories of mankind got passed along [...] for all of us today to know who we are" (viii). The importance of invoking history here centers not only on the exorcism of its haunting specters but also in the maintenance of history's very presence incarnated within the black body. As Dyson puts it, "The true impact of Haley's book is that it started a conversation about black roots that continues to this day. DNA tests to determine black ancestry are more popular than ever" (xi).

Rodriguez's rejection of this literature and its politics makes visible two competing diagnoses about the fundamental problems of American society: one (the recognitional) based on the problem of "racial amnesia" ("forgetting" the past secures its perennial return), the other (the redistributive) highlighting the continued struggle between labor and capital that necessitates, at the very least, union advocacy. Although Haley's fictive effort to trace his lineage led him to the "crumbling ruins" of a slave fort in Africa,[29] Rodriguez provokingly asserts instead, "Aztec ruins hold no special interest for me. I do not search Mexican graveyards for ties to unnamable ancestors" (3). *Roots* and its reception enable a recognitional view of the problems affecting American life: the persistence of the effects of slavery, the necessity of testimony, and the importance of speaking the names of the deceased. *Roots* and other works like it produce the grounds for a shared culture and identity and, therefore, effectively occlude the fundamental differences between people that Rodriguez insists on maintaining. Only by identifying this difference and registering it as a problem – "difference" being the result of material deprivation – is its attempted neutralization possible.

5 Recognitional Witnessing versus Redistributive Representation: *I, Rigoberta Menchú* (1984)

Rodriguez's critique of Chicano organic intellectuals and the representational claims they advanced was not the only one available during this time. Chicana feminists critiqued the Chicano Movement for foregrounding male leadership and marginalizing the experiences of women. Not seeing themselves represented by the self-proclaimed Chicano leaders, writers including Cherríe Moraga and Gloria Anzaldúa, who co-edited the influential collection *This Bridge Called My Back* (1981), sought competing modes of expression to circumvent the problems that representation as such produces.[30] Describing these efforts, John Beverley argues that "Chicana feminist and lesbian writers like Gloria Anzaldúa, are using poetry and narrative to redefine and reenergize a previously male-centered identity politics, preparing the ground for the emergence of new forms of liberation struggle" (*Against* xiii).

Beverley tellingly connects these efforts to a genre that came into prominence during this time in the form of Rigoberta Menchú's testimonio. Published after *Hunger of Memory*, *I, Rigoberta Menchú: An Indian Woman in Guatemala* (1984) was often contrasted to Rodriguez's text and politics. Whereas he

---

[29] I say "fictive" because of the controversy surrounding Haley's novel. Harold Courlander sued Haley for plagiarizing his novel *The African* (1967). The suit led to a financial settlement and apology by Haley. See Stanford's article, "Roots and Grafts on the Haley Story."

[30] See Arellano's "The Borders of the Frame."

refused to represent the voices of others, for Beverley, Menchú presents the voice of the poor by allowing the poor – embodied by Menchú – to speak directly (bracketing the controversy concerning the authenticity of the account).[31] Beverley understood the testimonio as moving beyond conservative concepts such as the "author," "authorial intention," and "literature."[32] As an ideological construct, literature "had a central role in the self-representation of the upper and upper-middle strata of Latin American society; it was one of the social practices by which such strata constituted themselves as dominant" (*Against* ix). Literature helped enable a social hierarchy that produces a horizontal "position of enunciation" that reflects the view elites had of themselves (*Against* 18). Even if "progressive intellectuals" wanted to speak for the "popular masses" in good faith to enunciate their needs, literature's vertical model of representation inevitably compromised their efforts (*Against* 17). Yet, for Beverley, the testimonio circumvents the problem of "vertical representation" by maintaining the integrity of the speaker's identity.

Beverley defines the testimonio as "a novel or novella-length narrative in book or pamphlet (i.e., graphemic as opposed to acoustic) form, told in the first person by a narrator who is also the real protagonist or witness of the events she or he recounts" (*Against* 70). His emphasis on "real" is crucial because it mitigates the need for representational mediation. As George Yúdice similarly argues, as an actual "witness," the speaker of a testimonio "portrays his or her own experience as an agent (rather than a representative) of a collective memory and identity" (17). The testimonio was "popular, oral discourse," instead of fictional literature (Yúdice 17). Its speaker "does not speak for or represent a community but rather performs an act of identity-formation" (Yúdice 42). A testimonio such as Menchú's does not *represent* the Guatemalan poor; the voice of her testimony *is* their voice. The *testimonio* produced an alternative horizontal "position of enunciation" capable of foreclosing the representational intermediaries (*Against* 18). For Beverley, Menchú could employ the mechanisms of the university (its editors, publishers, and readership) "without succumbing to an ideology of the literary generated and maintained by the university, or, what amounts to the same thing, without abandoning her identity as a member of her community" (*Against* 14). And by remaining true to her identity, she could remain true to her community, organically advancing their collective interests without the risk of cooptation or misrepresentation. The problem the testimonio appeared to solve is one that organic intellectuals faced when considering their ability to connect their work to the needs of the oppressed.

---

[31] See David Stoll's *Rigoberta Menchú and the Story of All Poor Guatemalans* (1999).
[32] See, for example, "The Margin at the Center," in Beverley's *Testimonio*, pp. 29–44.

As Eugenio Di Stefano argues, though, Menchú appears to be a conduit who presents a scene the way a camera does; she is "less as an agent who intends to represent these abuses" than she is "a witness whose *testimonio* captures these events (regardless of her intention). That is, the *testimonio*, like the camera, testified to her presence, to her pain, to the 'urgency of her situation' that crafting a poem, article, or a novel would delay if not impede" (91). Indeed, argues Di Stefano, photographs of atrocities achieve what critics such as Beverley and Yúdice claim the testimonio makes available: the seemingly unmediated re-presentation of a scene without resorting to representation. In this "fantasy," "the *testimonio* does not represent but is an unmediated opening into an event" (Di Stefano 91). To its academic advocates, the testimonio "brings us into the world of these violations, close to witnessing them, closer to the victim's pain" (Di Stefano90).

Yet, insofar as the testimonio is understood not as a "representation" but as an event that brings us closer to the speaker's pain, it might not matter what exactly Menchú *says* so long as the presence of her voice circulates. In a series of interviews with Elisabeth Burgos-Debray, Menchú told her story, which Burgos-Debray transcribed and then compiled into *Me llamo Rigoberta Menchú y así me nació la conciencia* (1983). According to Burgos, Menchú's testimonio was initially understood as "a political campaign, not anthropology or literature" (Stoll xi), a campaign meant to change international opinion about the efforts of the Guerrilla Army of the Poor against the Guatemalan army. By highlighting and circulating the first-person account of the "lower classes," the testimonio would "grant visibility to the oppressed, in the name of whom organic intellectuals would lead the revolution, which would occur through guerrilla warfare" (Stoll xi). Yet, the desire to neutralize the politics of representation by invoking the power of identity helps explain Burgos-Debray's paragraph-long description of the cultural authenticity of Menchu's attire, which evinces her authenticity as a spokesperson (Menchú and Burgos-Debray xiv). The authenticity of Menchú's voice can seemingly pierce through the many layers of mediation (Menchú provides her oral testimony in a language, Spanish, that is not her native tongue, which is then recorded and edited by Burgos-Debray, who is then translated by Ann Wright and circulated in the form of a book). Menchú's voice's "inner cadences are so pregnant with meaning that we actually seem to hear her speaking and can almost hear her breathing" (Menchú and Burgos-Debray xii). Her authentic voice/identity seems to figuratively transcend the mediation of representation itself, making Menchú's presence felt.

Despite her emphasis on the testimonio's political campaign, Burgos-Debray ultimately values Menchú's testimony on recognitional grounds. In her introduction to Menchú's testimonio, Burgos-Debray explicitly describes how "[Menchú] and her people are taken into account only when their labour power is needed; culturally, they are discriminated against and rejected [...] She is fighting for the recognition of her culture, for the acceptance of the fact that it is different and for her people's rightful share of power" (Menchú and Burgos-Debray xiii). While mentioning the exploitation of the indigenous' labor and the indigenous fight for power, the key term for Burgos-Debray is "culture," and the critical intervention to be made appears to be preservationist. Note the sheer recurrence of the term "culture" in Burgos-Debray's introduction:

> Her voice is so heart-rendingly beautiful because it speaks to us of every facet of the life of a people and their oppressed *culture*. But Rigoberta Menchú's story does not consist solely of heart-rending moments. Quietly, but proudly, she leads us into her own *cultural* world, a world in which the sacred and the profane constantly mingle, in which worship and domestic life are one and the same, in which every gesture has a pre-established meaning. Within that *culture*, everything is determined in advance; everything that occurs in the present can be explained in terms of the past and has to be ritualized so as to be integrated into everyday life, which is itself a ritual. (xii; emphasis added)

In this account, the persistence of Menchú's identity bespeaks the historical continuity of an indigenous way of life, the attempted eradication of which amounts to genocide insofar as it prohibits the continuity of an identity. Burgos-Debray thus highlights recognition as the necessary intervention: the recognition of the persistence of a cultural history. History, in this understanding, persists in the problems of the present, determining its contours. Such a recognitional account of the present-day relevance of cultural history is comparable to the prevalent notion of cultural identity that informs Haley's *Roots* and its reception. This understanding of the value of recognitional history ensures that the past is not forgotten so that its crimes can be addressed, its victims redeemed, and its lessons learned.

This emphasis of cultural history, though, could compromise Menchu's testimonio's politics by foregrounding cultural recognition instead of structural inequality. The tension between the text's explicit radical politics (its call for change) and its depiction of a culture (its call for cultural preservation) remains palpable, raising a question about *who* gets to appreciate a way of life. Readers can register the relevance of this question when, in her introduction, Burgos-Debray describes Menchú's "politeness" and "delicacy," which, she writes, are products of a culture that teaches "Indian children" the importance of "delicacy from a very early age; they begin to pick coffee when they are still very young and the berries have to be plucked with great delicacy if the branches are not to be damaged" (Menchú and Burgos-Debray xiv–xv). Menchú describes the necessity of introducing young children to the labor of picking coffee, which Burgos-Debray characterizes as a cultural rite of passage. Enjoying this culture *as a culture* requires conceptually bracketing it from the conditions that brought it into being. That is, a recognitional view of Menchú's testimonio results in the understanding of a way of life as culture that can be appreciated by those not having to live it.

We need only consider the difference between the Spanish and English titles of Menchú's testimonio to see how it became subsumed into the 1980s discourse of multiculturalism and cultural recognition. The Spanish title, *Me llamo Rigoberta Menchú y así me nació la conciencia*, should be translated as *My Name is Rigoberta Menchú, and This is How My Consciousness Was Born*, a title that highlights Menchú's political radicalization.[33] The testimonio, though, was published into English as *I, Rigoberta Menchú: An Indian Woman in Guatemala*, a title that excludes her critical political consciousness in favor of foregrounding her indigenous identity. Whereas the former title requires an understanding of the political realities that demand change (the redistributive), the latter is incorporated into the 1980s multicultural discourse that demands cultural appreciation (the recognitional).

Compare Beverley and Yúdice's account of the value of testimonial witnessing, to Bertolt Brecht's explanation of the importance of epic theater. Brecht explains epic theater via an especially relevant example involving an eyewitness of a traffic accident. He compares the eyewitness of an accident to an actor on stage performing for a group of onlookers, the theater's audience. The eyewitness/actor stages the accident for the audience but does so in a way that ensures that the audience understands that they are watching a representation. The actor must continually convey to the onlookers/audience that "what you are seeing now is a repeat" (*Brecht* 121). There is no doubt that this actor "has been through an 'experience, but he is not out to make his demonstration serve as an 'experience' for the audience" (*Brecht* 122).

Whereas some understood the testimonio as making available an experience that brings the audience closer to the victim's pain, for Brecht, the actor "must not 'cast a spell over anyone'" (*Brecht* 121). The actor must avoid "presenting himself in such a way that someone calls out 'What a lifelike portrayal of a chauffeur!'" (*Brecht* 122). And whereas Menchú was understood as inextricably connected to the testimonio that makes her voice present, Brecht instead argues that the witness/actor must use "a somewhat complex technique to detach himself from the character portrayed" (*Brecht* 121). Brecht's eyewitness

---

[33] The radical pedagogue Paolo Freire would describe this "birth" as the start of Menchú's critical consciousness (her "*conscientização*").

must call attention to his status as an actor portraying a role, thereby making "plainly apparent" the "whole machinery" of the theater's means of representation (*Brecht* 122). For Brechtian epic theater, this means the exposure of the mechanisms of theater, the lighting, the staging, and the acting *as* acting.

The normative "point" of this distancing approach was the solicitation of interpretive judgment based on the understanding of what happened. Instead of an absorptive "experience," the audience is meant "to form an opinion about the accident" (*Brecht* 121). As Jennifer Ashton insightfully explains, "it's worth noting here that the [German] word that Brecht uses to capture what *is* 'the point,' '*Urteil*,' has strong juridical connotations of the kind that 'opinion' carries only in its more restricted uses."[34] For Brecht, then, such "demonstrations" "should have a socially practical significance," a "practical purpose," that aims "to portray social processes as seen in their causal relationships" (*Brecht* 121–2).

To say that the aesthetic that proved to be dominant during the 1980s was the recognitional does not capture the extent to which it proved to be as transnational as the neoliberal economy out of which it emerged. Studying the post-dictatorial Latin American literature published since the 1980s, Eugenio Di Stefano argues that the call for the protection of human rights replaced the political projects critical of dictatorial regimes.[35] Such calls for the protection of human rights were aided by literature that highlighted "torture, mutilations, and other corporeal injustice" perpetuated by the dictatorships in countries including Chile, Argentina, and Uruguay (Di Stefano 3). As crucial as these efforts to highlight atrocities were, they did not always provide the historical context explaining the causes of the atrocities themselves. Di Stefano argues that the literature and discourse of human rights seek to create an intense affective experience so that the pain of the tortured can be witnessed and felt.

Without the necessary causal understanding of the conditions leading to the atrocities themselves, such a strategy will be short-lived because it is based on the intensity of affective experiences devoid of a causal explanation of the problem's origins. Beholders are invited to identify and feel, but not necessarily to judge critically and understand. The publicization of human rights violations and horrifying atrocities can solicit a strong moral condemnation; but politics, understood as competing accounts explaining, say, the role of the state, need not come into play in the sense of choosing sides. Yet, for Brechtian theater, the point is the enabling of normative judgment to thereby find those responsible for

---

[34] See Ashton's "Poetry and the Price of Milk." Ashton's reading of Brecht's "Street Scene" has been invaluable to my understanding of the redistributive and its difference from the recognitional.

[35] For an elaboration of this point, see Striffler's *Solidarity* (2019).

what happened. The eyewitness/actor's "demonstration has a practical purpose," he argues, because it "intervenes socially" (*Brecht* 122). Social intervention, here, is identical to the inducement of judgment. Putting it more antagonistically, the point of judgment in Brecht's historical moment ("class war in its acutest and most terrible stage" [*Brecht* 121]) was the identification of the enemy to find them guilty.

6 Identifying the Enemy: Daniel James *Famous All Over Town* (1983)

Daniel James's controversial novel *Famous All Over Town* (1983) holds a transitional position in my literary-historical account because it explicitly acknowledges the value of testimony, and of coming to terms with history, while ultimately enabling the redistributive estrangement we have seen in Brecht. The novel's plot focuses on a young fourteen-year-old boy named Rudy "Chato" Medina, who lives in a Los Angeles Mexican American neighborhood with his parents and siblings. Yet, the novel begins with the older Chato returning to what had been his childhood neighborhood but is now a large parking lot. Later in the novel, he recounts how he forces himself to witness the painful destruction of the neighborhood, saying to himself, "[s]top and look even if it hurts [...] Look hard so later you could testify" (278). His invocation of the importance of testimony resonates with the novel's epigraph taken from Bernal Díaz del Castillo's sixteenth-century eyewitness account of the Aztec empire before its destruction: "But of the wonders that I then beheld, today all is overthrown and lost and nothing is left standing." Díaz del Castillo's testimony of a culture destroyed by Spanish colonial expansion resonates with Chato's present-day injustices perpetuated against Mexicans and Mexican Americans living in the United States. As Chato recalls how the bulldozers raze the houses on his block, he says his address aloud as a form of incantation that brings his memories into being, memories that constitute the novel's flashback plot.

The novel's conceit thus presents the protagonist as a testimonio figure who relates his story. Chato "spoke the magic word" and creates an incantatory experience for the reader to witness his tragic life (7). Just as nothing remains of the Aztec buildings' splendor, except for their textual depiction, Chato's spoken account can, at the very least, circulate and resist being relegated to oblivion. And just as Michael Eric Dyson's reading of *Roots* leads to his diagnosis of the paradigmatic American malady, "the long midnight of slavery's haunting presence" (xi), *Famous* appears to suggest the necessity of grappling with the long history of Spanish colonization.

But, in a crucial detail of this opening scene, the antagonist Chato identifies – "the enemy," as he puts it (7) – is the Southern Pacific Railroad. Through coercion and brute institutional strength, this corporation, as an entity within the economy, decimates Chato's neighborhood to make a large parking lot for its trailers, which it needs to help circulate goods in an increasingly globalized market. The enemy is not racial or national; it is economic. And even as the novel's plot places Chato in the position of an eyewitness narrating his story, it draws attention to his status *as* a narrator. The novel's complex narrative temporality forces readers to question the setting and the narrator's place within it. The novel begins with a twenty-eight-year-old Chato, who tells a story of his fourteen-year-old self that ends with his arrest for being a graffiti artist, "a writer," as the arresting officer describes him (284). The novel's last sentences end the novel abruptly, quickly flashing forward to a narrative present in which Chato appears to speak directly to the reader: "In case you are curious, you could possibly read all about it someday. When and if I ever get around to writing it down, that is" (285). If readers are to understand this temporal setting as matching the novel's opening, an older Chato reflecting on his troubled life, we know that he never does get to "writing it down" – he speaks his narrative aloud. So how does the reader have access to his narrative? Where do readers stand relative to Chato's enunciation? How does he get his story published? What are the institutional mechanisms in place for such narratives to be published and circulated? It is almost as if Daniel James assumes the pseudonym Danny Santiago to appear to be more "organic" to Chato's identity and, therefore, able to transcribe his testimonio without being charged with cooptation and self-interest.

By thematizing the act of storytelling throughout the novel, James appears to foresee his eventual exposure and preemptively addresses the issue in the novel's plot. Chato recalls how when his mother went into labor, his oldest sister, Lena, called for the doctor, pointedly lying about their family name on the phone. For Lena, lying is a way to circumvent racism and get a doctor to treat a Mexican woman. She tells Chato, "If our name was O'Toole or Shitzenheim the damn doctor would be on his way already" (19). Her mocking mention of the Irish and Jewish names suggests her understanding of ethnic hierarchies within the twentieth-century United States. The Irish and Jewish, who had also faced discrimination as immigrants to the country, are nevertheless more "white" than Mexicans and, thus, less likely to encounter racist discrimination. "They never believe you if you tell the truth," she advises Chato, suggesting that her lie is not malicious so much as expedient. Her mother does, after all, require urgent care. By changing some biographical facts about herself, she obtained the necessary attention from her audience. Whereas a Mexican American character lies to get help, the novel's far more privileged white author lies to get published. Yet, James' self-serving machination produces a novel that thematizes the value of truth-telling *via fiction*. Insofar as "they" will "never believe you if you tell the truth," lying can be an expedient path to getting others to understand the precarious situation involving Mexican Americans living in East Los Angeles.

This "truth" made available via fiction certainly involves exposing the anti-Mexican biases of healthcare professionals and the law. This is why the character Lena anticipates that the dispatch operator would consider her a "dirty Mexican" if she knew her last name was Medina (20). She also knows that when a police officer shot Chato's friend in the back, it could have been her brother Chato who was shot (175). The callousness with which the police handle Mexican Americans earns them the nickname "Babykillers" (183), and those attending the funeral of the slain young Mexican American suspect that the police "didn't respect" him (183). Indeed, they suspect, "They shot him because he was a Mexican" (183). At the funeral, the anger over this racism erupts into a riot wherein the mourners damage the funeral home. Whereas the police officer who killed Chato's friend eventually gets away with a mild reprimand, the mourners' actions at the funeral home earn them a dismissive verdict by the funeral home owner: They had "No respect! No culture!" (184).

The depicted riot – caused by anger over state-sanctioned violence against people of color – is far too familiar to our post-2020 eyes. The novel, though, appears to insist that the truth of the situation is not merely one involving individuals' racial biases. Concerned about a drop in his grades, Chato's sympathetic counselor asks him to respond to a series of tests, including Rorschach images, by "mak[ing] up a little story to fit them" (67), The counselor places fourteen-year-old Chato in an author role, and Chato revealingly produces what he considers "good stories [...] with lots of action" (67). The counselor finds the stories alarmingly violent, asking Chato why he does not instead produce stories with "happy endings" (67). Chato's response again invokes the question of truth relative to fiction. Referring to the examination pictures, Chato says, "That's a sad bunch of pictures [...] so why lie about it?" (67). When the counselor points out that he himself does not find the picture cards sad, Chato offers a reason why: "You're not a Mexican" (67). The dramatic irony of this statement – "You're not a Mexican" – is compounded by the fact that it was written by a white author and ventriloquized through a Mexican American character.[36] One way to read these lines within this scene is to suggest that the identity of the speaker *matters* in questions relating to the

---

[36] As Marcial González argues, Daniel James must have recognized the irony of this statement as he wrote it (115).

truth, so much so that only "a Mexican" like Chato could know what it is like to live in his neighborhood. But another reading could register the *discrepancy* between what Chato claims and what readers understand. Chato claims to be producing a story that is adequate to the images. The truth of the psychology tests, however, is that there is no "true" narrative, only what is projected by the observer. By noting the discrepancy between what Chato thinks and what the reader knows, one can see how sadness and violence are not features of the test's images but are, rather, projections of Chato's state of mind. In other words, the problem here (violence) is not structural (about the images themselves) but, rather, perspectival (about Chato), the solution thus requiring a change in his attitude. But – and this difference makes all the difference – unlike the psychology tests, the social problems the novel depicts are not created by its writer's (or the novel's readers') projected emotions. The novel shows that insofar as one wants a change in perspective within children like Chato, one would need to change the structural context in which children like him are raised.

By placing Chato in the position of an author figure who creates "good stories" with "lots of action," *Famous* highlights Chato's position as *a narrator*. Chato, here, is not simply a point of identification for the reader, wherein the reader – like the sympathetic high school counselor – identifies with his plight or feels bad for his tragic life. *Famous*, here, insists that readers consider Chato as a narrator within a novel, within a meaningful narrative structure that thematically highlights the very efficacy of novels to dramatize the shortcomings of recognition. Readers need only assess the high school counselor's proposed solution to Chato's situation. The well-intentioned counselor encourages Chato to develop his ethnic sense of self to make it to college. When Chato has the opportunity to visit Mexico with his family, the counselor enthusiastically encourages him to go: "What an opportunity, [Chato]. The temples of your ancestors, the land of your fathers, you'll see them with your own eyes" (205). The counselor describes his own trip to "the Promised Land," in which he "banged his head against the Wailing Wall and learned to be a Jew again" (205). Just as a trip to Sinai reinforced the counselor's Jewish identity, "[o]ne day in Mexico," he argues, could teach Rudy more about himself than "six whole months" of a class on Mexican history ever could (205). This is why the counselor advises Rudy to not "miss the pyramids": "Find your roots! Discover your identity!" (205). The novel seems to satirize the counselor's advice concerning his head-banging self-discovery while nevertheless recognizing its well-intentioned practicality. The overly enthusiastic counselor, who is "busy shouting" and has to "run his fingers through his hair to calm down," might be a bit "crazy," as Rudy's sister puts it, but "he likes" Mexican American students (205). He relates to Chato, describing his own impoverished childhood in the run-down tenements of New York and its antisemitic public school system. "We won our A's in spite of them," he pronounces (68). "We made it," he tells Chato, enumerating the many Jewish lawyers and doctors that came out of the tenement (68). The counselor's encouraging narrative is that of perseverance in the face of adversity, the narrative of the upward-class mobility enabled by changing one's perspective and "cooperating." In short, by becoming a proud Mexican, Chato can begin to advance to the middle class.

The novel thus explicitly connects the utility of narratives of ethnic identity to narratives of upward-class mobility. Had Chato seen the pyramids, he may have considered his ancestors worthy of his respect instead of thinking about them as historical "losers" (247). While in Mexico, Chato had begun to learn that his ancestors had been "famous all over Mexico for the clay pots and idols they made" (246), the phrase, "famous all over Mexico," echoing Chato's titular desire to be "famous all over town" through his graffiti (284). If only Chato identified with these ancestors and channeled his creative energy into a more productive form of cultural expression (if only Chato became, say, a writer of fiction instead of a writer of graffiti; 284), he too could have "made it." But just as identification is not enabled by a story about Mexican Americans, Chato also misses an opportunity to connect with his ancestors because his father decides not to take the family to see the pyramids. At the last minute, Chato's father passes the highway exit (256).

This foreclosure of a potential scene of identity affirmation simultaneously appears as a lost opportunity that is ultimately beside the point. *Famous All Over Town's* ambition instead parallels Chato's desire when Chato writes his name on the walls of his neighborhood; he imagines how his name will bother "the vice president of Bank of America [...] like a toothache" (283–284). Discomfiture – not identification – is the point of Chato's graffiti and James' novel. Like the infamous "protest novel," *Native Son* by Richard Wright, through which Wright sought to preclude the sympathetic identification that might elicit "tears of banker's daughters" (*Native Son* 454), *Famous* tries to perturb the bankers themselves, thereby critiquing the political economy that values and protects bankers and the institutions they serve at the expense of its most vulnerable citizens. Like Wright, who became disenchanted with the Communist Party but learned the value of "using words as a weapon, using them as one would use a club" (*Black Boy* 248), James had also been associated with the Communist Party. Even though James came to say that he "got rid of the 1930s Marxist insistence on art as a social weapon" (as quoted in González 117), *Famous* is meant to be affecting in precisely this way: as a toothache that hurts.

Famous connects this discomfort to causal understanding by continually foregrounding its representational status and foreclosing the narrative ease of identification. When Chato is in juvenile detention, he is examined by doctors who give him notebooks "to do [his] writing in" (285). The doctors, tellingly, are "not crazy about" what he writes (285). The examining doctors would like to read stories that affirm a view of a well-adjusted young man who fits into society; Chato, however, writes stories that reveal a problem in society that precludes this adjustment. The reader of Chato's stories must face the discomfiting realization that readerly easy and sympathetic identification will not help solve his problems.

Famous thus highlights the distinction between a well-intentioned idealism about the power of reading ethnic literature in a school setting and the everyday realities of living in poverty. The teacher, initially, is all about "preaching Democracy in the Classroom and Everybody Express Yourself." She drops this preaching when "one day somebody stole $11" from her purse (74). The students' situation is dire, and they, understandably, want a way out of it.[37] One of the savviest students in the school, Eddie Velasquez, considers the value of reading novels in an English class (one of "those bullshit courses"; 72) only in terms of an opportunity to earn an easy grade. Grades, he foresees, will clear the path to his own office and a position as a certified public accountant (73). Eddie, who does not appear to understand the point of reading a novel, is ironically assigned to tutor Chato in English. Eddie's inadequate tutoring, though, reveals that Eddie's savviness *does* correspond with the ultimate lesson the teacher wants her students to learn. Eddie suspects that literature teachers "expect something way bigger, like Attitude to Life" (72). Moments later, Chato's teacher affirms this suspicion when she suggests that Mexican Americans can "identify with" Mexican American characters, "And learn from their experiences ... Isn't that a better way for us to deal with Discrimination?" (75). Her desire to use ethnicity as a bridge between her students and the characters appears hollow as she recites a reading of the assigned novel that ultimately affirms Eddie's shortsighted understanding. For her, after all, the point does seem to be about character building that will enable those like Eddie to pull themselves out of their situation, presumably, by their proverbial bootstraps.

This interpretive realization of the ironic discrepancy between the characters' understanding and that of the reader again reveals the difference between the recognitional account of the value of literature and its redistributive critique. *Famous* invites readers to consider the function of literature about Mexican Americans, portraying two possibilities. In one recognitional possibility, Mexican American literature could offer uplifting narratives of perseverance

---

[37] Their junior high school, as Chato's counselor puts it, operates more like a "penitentiary" than a school, replete with "Fences! Policemen in the restrooms!" (68).

and progress explicitly connected with identity and upward mobility. James could have written a recognitional novel with a happy ending; he could have produced a novel (similar to the assigned short about the character, Pancho) by making his protagonist be Eddie Velasquez, a student whose ambitious attitude helps clear the way to a job as an accountant. The optimism of this novel's potential happy ending, like the advice given to Chato by his school's counselor, would have highlighted the importance of perseverance made possible through the power of his reinforced ethnic identity.

Alternatively, a redistributive understanding would instead present Mexican American literature as offering provocative narratives that affect like weapons by discomfiting readers. Such a redistributive narrative would call the existing structure into question. This is why James wrote a novel whose protagonist is Chato (not Eddie), who would consider the recognitional version of his story to be a lie about the grim reality so many Mexican Americans face. A recognitional story of a strengthened identity that promotes perseverance would suggest that the problem Mexican Americans face is one of perspective and grit, the solution being a sense of self reinforced through Mexican American literature. This suggestion would further imply that the publishing of more novels about Mexican Americans would help the most impoverished. Given the logic of James's novel, this suggestion would be a lie indeed.

7 Recognitional Novels: Arturo Islas *The Rain God* (1984)

Insofar as I am attempting to provide a way of understanding two distinct aesthetics within Mexican American literature of the early 1980s, some of my readers might object to my selection of texts. Why revisit Richard Rodriguez, who has explicitly ostracized himself from Mexican American letters? Why include Daniel James, whose relation to Mexican American literature could justifiably be characterized as exploitative? The writer, Arturo Islas, helps provide answers. Islas felt compelled to respond to both Rodriguez and James, explicitly connecting *Hunger of Memory* and *Famous All Over Town* as examples of the type of literature taken seriously by major publishers. Writing before James' identity was exposed, Islas takes stock of recent Mexican American publications, noting what kind of work was being published by more prominent publishing houses. He writes to his editor:

> Look at this pathetic fact: in the last two years, the 'major' presses have published two books by writers of Mexican heritage born and brought up and educated in this country. One of them [Richard Rodriguez] hates his heritage and capitalizes on the backlash against affirmative action and bilingual programs; the other [Daniel James] writes about victimized, absolutely

helpless Mexicans in a barrio. And <u>that</u> is the image the rest of the country gets of Mexican-Americans and Chicanos. I know it doesn't bother you as much as it bothers me and the <u>rest</u> of us who do <u>not</u> fall into either category and who have been working our asses off all our lives to rise above such stereotype [sic]. I am completely demoralized. (as quoted in Cutler 96)

Islas rejects both *Hunger* and *Famous* as poor writing. His rejection invites readers to consider what, in his estimation, the literature written by Mexican Americans *should* be. What should this literature look like, if not what Rodriguez and James produced? In this section, I turn to Islas' novel *The Rain God* (1984), which I argue presents his view of what Mexican American literature could be. By comparing his aesthetic to what he rejects, we can better understand what is at stake in his aesthetic when compared to theirs.

Islas was irritated by the success of *Famous* and *Hunger* and the more modest reception of his first novel, *The Rain God*. He fictionalizes a response to the novel's tepid success in a sequel titled *Migrant Souls* (1990). The narrative voice describes the novelist's frustration over the reception of his novel titled *Tlaloc*, the name the Aztecs gave to their "rain god,":

> A modest, semi-autobiographical work, [the novel *Tlaloc*] was published by a small California press that quickly went out of business. *Tlaloc* was an academic, if not commercial, success and its author became known as an ethnic writer. After seeing what the world did to books, he returned humbly to the classroom and to criticism [. . .] The dumb sociologists want only positive images, whatever they are, from fiction writers. As if the whole world, especially their own little one, were one big happy collection of ethnic groups. (211)

The Rain God, like the fictional novel *Tlaloc,* was indeed published by a small Californian press (Alexandrian) that did, in fact, go out of business. Yet, the fictionalized novelist's frustration appears to reverse the irritation Islas expressed to his editor. If, for Islas, Rodriguez did not advance positive images of his heritage and James trafficked in negative stereotypes, here, the novelist rejects the view that his literature should merely produce positive ethnic depictions.

Yet, the seeming tension between the block quotations presents what a consistent view. Combined, the quotations offer the view that the representation of a people should exceed the sociological particularities besetting their lives. Some writers render a people as merely sociologically reactionary, unable to change their situation. Other writers, though, produce only positive images, thereby reducing literature to simplistic propaganda, the force of which also depends on sociological concerns. Islas' complaint, in short, is evaluative. Works like *Famous* and *Hunger* were, put simply, *not good* because they adhered to sociological views of Mexican Americans. Islas may appear to recall the Chicano rejection of the social sciences I discussed in Section 2. Yet he departs from the earlier Chicano novelists because he does not want to counteract one set of depictions with another more positive set. He wants to let his novels exist on the terms they establish for themselves and be evaluated on artistic grounds, separate from sociological concerns.

The Rain God should thus be understood as demonstrating Islas' attempts to deliver what a good Mexican American novel should offer. *The Rain God* thematizes the writing of novels, its protagonist being a college literature professor and novelist. The first scene depicts Miguel Angel (called "Miguel Chico") sitting in his study and looking at a photograph of himself and his grandmother, Encarnación Olmeca ("Mama Chona"). The narrative intermittently returns to this initial setting, suggesting that the novel's plot (like the plot of James' *Famous*) takes place within the protagonist's memory as he reflects on his relation to his family. Unlike *Famous*, however, Miguel Chico has "made it" through his college education. And, like Richard Rodriguez, who considers the extent to which his college education separates him from his family, Miguel Chico wonders if "he was still [. . .] an extension of them, the way a seed continues to be a part of a plant after it has assumed its own form which does not all resemble its origin, but which, nevertheless, is determined by it" (25). Although he realizes that he "had survived severe pruning," he wonders "if human beings, unlike plants, can water themselves" (26).

The answer, the novel suggests, is *no*. In a sentence that reads as a direct response to Rodriguez's *Hunger*, the retrospective narrator can look back on the younger, naive Miguel Chico and realize how "[i]n his arrogance, Miguel believed he was finding ways out of it through his university education. He had not yet had time to combine learning with experience, however, and he still felt himself superior to those who had brought him up and loved him" (91). Having received a formal education that enabled him to think he can leave his past behind him, Miguel Chico must confront the inescapability of his family's determinative influence on who he will always be.

The Rain God's conceit presents the novel as its protagonist's efforts to write a story that does not reject his family's influence. Unlike James' Chato, who creates "sad stories" (because, as he puts it, he "is Mexican") (*Famous* 67), the stories Miguel Chico produces end up being "happier than their 'real' counterparts" (24). Miguel Chico attributes this penchant for happy endings to his grandmother's rejection of what she considers to be the seedier parts of life. Her selective idealism includes her attempted erasure of the Mexican and Indian parts of her identity. She "refused to associate [. . .] with anything Mexican or Indian because it was somehow impure" (27), and she "had taught all her children that [members of her family] were better than the illiterate riffraff from across the river" (15). The novel's self-commentary on the fictive conditions of its production thus depicts Miguel Chico's coming to terms with his family, their assimilation, and their snobbery. He begins to learn that the supposedly illiterate Mexicans and Indians are not inferior, nor are they persons apart; they partially constitute his family's genealogy (however much this lineage is denied), and his family, in turn, determines him.

Miguel Chico comes to terms with what Rodriguez described as the supposedly "unnameable ancestors" who created the "Aztec ruins" (*Hunger* 3). Such ancestors remain unnamed, *The Rain God* implies, because writers like Rodriguez refuse to offer the dead a textual conduit for their presence. Recall that Rodriguez pointedly states, "Aztec ruins hold no special interest for me" (3). Recall, too, how *Famous* telling forecloses scenes of ethnic reunification by visiting the pyramids in Mexico. Although Chato could have visited the ruins of his ancestors, James' plot will ensure that he misses his chance. *The Rain God*, though, ensures that its protagonist visits the pyramids in Mexico, where he experiences a sense of unification. While at Teotihuacan, he encounters just what Chato's counselor suggests Chato would: Miguel Chico "felt the presence of the civilizations that had constructed them [...] his ancestors" (26). The sublimity of this experience at the pyramids, his simultaneous awe and terror, recurs toward the end of the novel, when, awakened by a nightmare, he begins to write. "He needed very much to make peace with his dead," he realizes. "He would feed them words and make his candied skulls out of paper" (160). The reference to the *Día de los Muertos* ritual converts the act of writing into an offering that honors and propitiates the dead by feeding them. If writing keeps the dead at bay, it also provides the medium for bringing them into being by representing them.

Unlike Rodriguez's rejection of indigenous ancestry, *The Rain God* imagines the textual conduit through which the dead can be honored and connected to the present. The novel includes a meaningfully resonant quotation of a fifteenth-century poem written by the Aztec poet, King Netzahualcoyotl. Transcribed by one of Miguel Chico's relatives, Netzahualcoyotl's poem describes the inevitable ephemerality of human achievement. Describing the magnificent ruins at Teotihuacan, which neighbored Netzahualcoyotl's city-state, Netzahualcoyotl states, the "once animate bodies of men who sat upon their thrones" become "pestilential dust [...] Vanished are these glories" (as quoted in *Rain* 162). *The Rain God*'s quotation of the poem, however, stops at its more optimistic line: "Nothing recalls them but the written page" (162). Dead bodies wither into dust, but the printed word reanimates their spirit. Indeed, present-day readers know about Netzahualcoyotl and his belief in Tlaloc (the "Rain God") because of the written word. Much less is known about the "ancestors" who built the pyramids of Teotihuacan and predate Nezahualcoyotl by centuries. The presence of the Teotihuacan pyramids stands as testimony of their creation, yet the names of their creators remain textually absent.

This longing to commune with the ancestral dead – and their textual resuscitation – also animates *The Rain God*'s epigraph, taken from Pablo Neruda's epic poem, *Canto General*. In the canto, "*Las Alturas de Macchu Picchu*," the poet describes travelling to the magisterial Incan site, "the dwelling of what earth / never covered in vestments of sleep" (Felstiner and Neruda 85). Like Teotihuacan, Machu Picchu's endurance bespeaks the absence of its inhabitants: "Stone upon stone, and man, where was he?" wonders the poet. "Macchu Picchu, did you set stone upon stone on a base of rags?" (95). Here, the poet speaks to the site because of "man's" absence. Whereas the ruins may remain "never covered" by earth and sleep, such was not the fate of its builders "because everything, clothing, skin, jars, / words, wine, bread, / is gone, fallen to earth" (85). The imaginative capacity of the poetic vision, however, does end up seeing "the ancient human, a human slave, sleeping / in the fields," while the poetic voice's rhetorical power imagines the dead's resuscitative awakening. Here is Islas' translation of the canto's crescendo that serves as *The Rain God*'s epigraph:

> *I come to speak through your dead mouths . . .*
> *Give me silence, water, hope.*
> *Give me struggle, iron, volcanoes.*
> *Fasten your bodies to me like magnets.*
> *Hasten to my veins, to my mouth.*
> *Speak through my words and my blood.*

The epigraph presents a representational problem and provides the imaginative means to circumvent it. The poet's ambition, here, is to speak for the dead by providing the conduit through which he can imagine the dead speaking for themselves. Blood becomes an unbreakable link to the past, and writing is the fictive technology enabling the past's emergence in the present.

The Rain God, then, thematizes the development of this fictive technology by operating as a kind of spirit medium. The novel depicts how Nina, the godmother of the novelist protagonist Miguel Chico, does not enjoy reading novels because, as she puts it, novelists tend to focus on the "endless suffering of southern belles" (41). "Why don't they write about us?" she asks her sister, to which her sister, in turn, asks, "Who wants to read about Mexicans? We're not glamorous enough. We just live" (41). Just living, though, is precisely what interests Nina, who finds "daily life and real people [...] infinitely more interesting" than the depicted trials and tribulations of "southern belles" (41). Although Nina dislikes novels, tellingly, she learns to enjoy séances, during which she once experienced the presence of her dead mother and sister (34). For Nina, séances, unlike novels, are about "us" and families "just living" even when the "us" in question have already died. The type of narrative Nina *would* enjoy, *The Rain God* implies, is the kind that its protagonist would come to write: A novel that creates the fictive technology through which something like the return of the dead can be imagined.

So, whereas Netzahualcoyotl's poem invokes and recalls those who "decided cases, presided in council, / commanded armies, conquered provinces" (as quoted in *Rain* 162), Miguel Chico (like Islas) instead writes about his family. The testimonial ambition that motivates *The Rain God* thus assumes a heightened ethical role because the dead that the novel metaphorically calls back are ordinary people (not statesmen or army commanders). After having almost died of intestinal cancer, Miguel Chico wonders if "perhaps he had survived to tell others about Mama Chona and people like Maria," his Mexican nanny, both of whom pass away during the course of the novel (28). Thus, Miguel Chico's writing is about the people Nina wants to see portrayed, and by representing the spiritual return of characters that die during the course of the plot (including the symbolic return of Miguel's dead uncle, Felix), *The Rain God* functions as a kind of metaphorical séance, enabling the figurative spiritual return and reconciliation of his family.

Islas' novel, then, negates Rodriguez's argument about the unavoidable difference between middle-class novelists and the poor subjects they represent. By writing a novel about a novelist who reaffirms his connection to his family and to his ancestors, he negates Rodriguez's critique of the middle-class focus of novels and of the supposed irrelevance of ancestral legacies on the present. Novels, in the view Islas makes available, can be a conduit for the voices of the dead so that their names are not forgotten while their stories remain told. This testimonial function explains why the novel's conclusion loops back to the initial scene. Miguel Chico, now a professor and writer, recalls Mama Chona's deathbed utterance: "*La familia*" (180). If, at the end of the novel's plot, such an utterance could be understood by the younger Miguel as cryptic, the older novelist and professor will use it as an injunction to guide his novel. Miguel Chico's status as an educated professor – should he let it – could function as the moral equivalent of Mama Chona's disdain towards Mexicans and Indians. Miguel Chico's position as a writer, though, serves the ethical function of testimony and recuperation. As a novelist, he can represent those who are not portrayed in literature, which tends to focus on, say, southern belles – not Mexican women.

There is the risk, though, that Islas' novel displaces the economic realities that beset the lives of the portrayed. By converting Rodriguez's *political* point about economic inequality into a psychological and ethical point about self-acceptance and the importance of maintaining familial ties, Islas risks conflating the problems of exploitation and economic inequality with the sins of condescension and snobbery. If the problem is snobbery, then the solution could be humility and reconciliation. This solution can appear to be made available by a recognitional novel that insists on familial unity against the snobbery of self-isolation. If novelists worry that their status separates them from the subjects they depict, a recognitional novel such as *The Rain God* provides a way to mitigate class difference. What is required is the comforting (self) acceptance that the novelist, as an integral part of the people he or she represents, is not so different after all.

For John Alba Cutler, Islas' *The Rain God* presents a more progressive work than Rodriguez's neoliberal *Hunger*. For Cutler, the comfortable fit of Rodriguez's writing in classes that teach undergraduates the language of corporate management suggests that the use of Rodriguez is a form of "soft multiculturalism" that suits the needs of the future managerial class: "multiculturalism as diversity management" (107). By using only "the voice of masculine disinterestedness," Rodriguez helps to consolidate the official exclusionary voice of the public sphere (95). Islas' commitment to representing the voice of others expands the otherwise monolithic Western literary canon by diversifying its discourses and modes of address. *The Rain God*, argues Cutler, "suggests strategies for *redistributing* literary cultural capital" (116; original emphasis). This redistributive effort demonstrates the novel's "literary multiculturalism" that can critique a Western-centric ideal of cultural capital (116).

What, we must ask, does "redistribution" mean here? Given his account of cultural capital redistribution, Cutler would need to show how the study of "hard" multiculturalism could be seen as existing in an adversarial relationship with the political economy. If a certain kind of English remains the language of the managerial class, how might a more diverse form of English prove to work against the logic of the market? The "culture wars" of the 1980s and 1990s demonstrated that the diversification of the canon was not ultimately a critique of the coterminous development of neoliberalism. It remains unclear how a more nuanced multiculturalist discourse would differ. Recall how, in Section 5, the recognitional focus on Rigoberta Menchú's identity occludes the economic and political causes of her exploitation and how the very inclusion of Menchú's testimonio on college syllabi was understood on recognitional terms. In 1988, Stanford made national news for updating its Western Civilization course, a first-year humanities requirement, to include texts such as Menchú's testimonio. As a journalist covering the incident describes, Stanford became the "Fort Sumter of the academic culture wars – the place where the first shot was fired in the battle between the protectors of Dante and Descartes and the promoters of diversity."[38] The alliteration of this framing helps emphasize what was at stake: On one hand are the dead white men, Dante and Descartes, on the other is "diversity."

When we use "redistribution" as a proxy for what amounts to a recognitional effort, redistribution amounts to the diversification of the beneficiaries of cultural capital, leaving the material problems of economic exploitation unaddressed. While the recognitional activism against discrimination and identity-based oppression remains necessary, antidiscrimination and antiracism cannot serve as entangled proxies for a redistributive politics. Just note how the Arlene Dávila acknowledges this fact:

> If I could reduce my decades-long studies on Latinx culture into one lesson, it is that *visibility* is merely the first step to *recognition*, which in turn, has very little to do with *equity*. Equity demands *structural and lasting transformation* in society, and in the context of the arts, in the makeup and functioning of all institutions that are part of the larger ecosystem of artistic evaluation – from art schools, to museums, to galleries, and more. (vii; emphasis added)

Restated in *Race Class*' terms, Dávila argues that the recognitional, which seeks visibility, has very little to do with the redistributive, which seeks structural change. So what, in Dávila's argument, *would* constitute such "structural and lasting transformation in society"? In her very next sentence, she frames the problem in terms of diversity: "Consider that as I write, and despite a mayoral mandate for art institutions to embrace diversity or risk losing funding, the staff at the New York City arts and culture institutions remains three-quarters white, even when whites represent only one quarter of the city's population" (vii). Although visibility is but one step toward recognition, and recognition has little to do with sustainable structural change, recognitional visibility, as embodied in the positions of influence, is presented as a solution.

8 The Culture of Poverty and the Program Era: Sandra Cisneros *The House on Mango Street* (1984)

Insofar as organic intellectuals' ability to represent others became understood as a problem to be solved, as we saw in Sections 3, 4, and 5, Islas portrays a solution. His novel depicts how an organic intellectual is not a person apart. He or she remains organically attached to family and community, the way a plant emerges out of a seed. This development continued the work of the previous generation's Chicanos, who had characterized the work of college professors and novelists as clearing the way toward justice. As we saw in

---

[38] Alison Schneider, *Stanford Revisits the Course That Set off the Culture Wars*, www.chronicle.com/article/stanford-revisits-the-course-that-set-off-the-culture-wars/.

Section 2, Chicano literature emerged, in part, to debunk the facile caricatures of "traditional" Mexican culture that supposedly prevented productive assimilation into the vaunted American "melting pot." I referred to David Riesman, Nathan Glazer, and Reuel Denney's *The Lonely Crowd* (1950) to highlight this view. Chicano literature, in turn, rejected the description of Mexican and Mexican American culture as "pathological," what Oscar Lewis called "a culture of poverty" in 1959.

My last extended example, Sandra Cisneros' *The House on Mango Street* (1984), was published the same year as *The Rain God,* at a time when the social sciences and popular discourses continued to circulate negative depictions of Mexican and Mexican American culture. As the Reagan administration continued to shift discussions of social welfare to the conservative right, *Mango Street* deals with the images of what then came to be referred to as the so-called "underclass."[39] When poor women, and especially poor women of color, were mentioned in popular discourse, they were often characterized as "welfare queens" taking advantage of government-funded programs. Cisneros, like the Chicano writers before her, turned to literature to expose these accounts as false.

Unlike Chicanos, however, Cisneros does not delineate a collective productive culture meant to foster the reader's pride.[40] According to John Alba Cutler, Cisneros offers a "powerful counter-discourse to culture-of-poverty theory by imagining the dynamic and complex inner lives of poor women of color" (121).

---

[39] Doug Glasgow's *The Black Underclass* (1980) and Ken Auletta's *The Underclass* (1982) anticipated arguments found in Lawrence M. Mead's *Beyond Entitlement: The Social Obligations of Citizenship* (1986) and William Julius Wilson's *The Truly Disadvantaged: The Inner City, the Underclass, and Public Policy* (1987). What started with Nixon's revision of the welfare system in the early 1970s – a revision praised by Glazer and Moynihan – led the way to systematic overhauls by the Reagan and Clinton administrations. Bill Clinton's 1992 presidential campaign's promise to "end welfare as we know it" was founded on the rhetoric of the "underclass." Once elected, Clinton made sure to target poor mothers and morally chastise "absent fathers." His reform of welfare culminated in the 1996 Personal Responsibility and Work Opportunity Act, effectively reversing a commitment to help impoverished children and their mothers. Advancing a narrative of pathology and self-help, politicians (following the conclusions of sociologists) urged the poor to follow their upper-class models and learn the ways of life more conducive to upward-class mobility.

[40] Indeed, *Mango Street*'s absorption into the multicultural discourse of the 1980s, included in syllabi as a way to expose students to a "Hispanic culture," is profoundly problematic. Insofar as the patriarchy evident in the novella's vignettes results from, as the young, inquisitive Esperanza puts it, "Mexicans" who "don't like their women strong" (10), readers should ask just what aspects of *Mango Street* get to count as the "Latino heritage" mentioned on the back cover of the 1991 Vintage Books edition: "Cisneros draws on her rich [Latino] heritage" (original brackets). This bizarrely decontextualized and edited quotation – taken from Bebe Moore Cambell's review not of *Mango Street* but of Cisneros' collection of short stories, *Woman Hollering Creek* (1991) – implies that *Mango Street* is as committed to exploring the richness and complexity of a Mexican heritage as Cisneros' later work. The inclusion of *The House on Mango Street* into the discourse of multiculturalism is misguided.

By depicting more sympathetic portrayals of women, he argues, *Mango Street* circulates a powerful response to the culture of poverty discourse that remained in heavy rotation during the 1980s. The women the novella represents are neither deviant nor aberrant; rather, they are in desperate need of help. *Mango Street*, dedicated to "*Las Mujeres*" (The Women), speaks on their behalf.

This effort was important because one of the co-authors of *The Lonely Crowd*, Nathan Glazer, went on to co-write two editions of *Beyond the Melting Pot* (1963, 1970). Glazer et al.'s text became one of the most influential accounts "explaining" how the melting pot theory of assimilation failed to describe why some ethnicities (namely, Puerto Ricans and African Americans) were less successful at assimilating and becoming upwardly mobile (their explanation being the paucity of certain ethnicities' cultures). *Beyond the Melting Pot*'s co-author, Daniel Patrick Moynihan, went on to serve as the Assistant Secretary of Labor, writing one of the most infamous re-articulations of Lewis' culture of poverty thesis. Published as *The Negro Family: The Case for National Action* (1965), the Moynihan Report, once again, attempted to explain why some ethnicities remain impoverished. Adolph Reed provides a list of problems Moynihan identifies as comprising the supposed "tangle of pathology" within African American culture, including "crime, drug abuse, teen-aged pregnancy, out-of-wedlock birth, female-headed households, and welfare dependency" (*Stirrings* 184). As this list of deviant sins begins to show, women play a central role in Moynihan's account. According to Moynihan, by becoming pregnant outside of an economically stable nuclear family, women become dependent on welfare and thereby lose the initiative to better themselves; and because women tend to be the head of nonnormative households, they cannot teach the next generation of men how to "be men," teaching them instead how to remain dependent on the state (42–43). These men will become the type of person who abuses and then abandons women (and so on). Poor women of color are thus, in effect, being blamed for the perpetuation of their poverty.

Mango Street's plot instead invites readers to contemplate the importance of literary testimony. On the last page of the novella, the young protagonist, Esperanza, imagines herself leaving her neighborhood and all of the women there in need of help. "One day I will pack my bags of books and paper," she states. "One day I will say goodbye to Mango" (110). Yet she will leave only to return. As she puts it, "I have gone away to come back. For the ones I left behind. For the ones who cannot out" (110). This concluding imaginative projection into Esperanza's future consolidates the efforts made by female characters who try to convince Esperanza to return. One such effort involves three mysterious women who, in a *Macbeth*-like prophecy scene, offer Esperanza the chance to make a wish. Unlike Shakespeare's witches who deliver three prophecies, the women simply assure Esperanza that her unspoken wish will come true and, three times, insist that she come back. "When you leave you must remember always to come back for the others," they tell her. "A circle, understand? [...] come back. For the ones cannot leave as easily as you" (105). Their prediction that she will leave does not foretell Shakespearean tragedy because their insistence that she return is optimistic. *Esperanza*, Spanish for "hope," could live up to her name and become a beacon to those still living on Mango Street.

One can begin to get a sense of why Esperanza would have to leave only to return – and how her homecoming will help those she leaves behind – by attending to the syntactical peculiarity of Esperanza's statements. Esperanza does not imagine herself packing her bags *full* of books and paper or *with* books and paper; she packs her bags *of* books and paper. It is as if the textual media constitute the very baggage enabling her departure. Mark McGurl's *The Program Era* provides one way of understanding this dynamic. Describing autopoetic circularity, he writes,

> To recover one's throne in the enchanted realm of one's own writing is to bend the arrow of personal experience around until it reattaches to its origin like a golden Möbius band. Instead of testifying to a permanent condition of disadvantage in the face of physical necessity [...] 'personal experience' is redeemed in this manner as a proud and vibrantly reflexive textual presence. (12)

Following McGurl, I suggest that Esperanza's emotional baggage, as it were, will become her enabling "baggage" by making possible her journey out of Mango Street and toward a future as a writer. As *The Program Era* persuasively shows, since the mid twentieth century, this path to becoming a writer has tended to lead to the creative writing programs housed in American institutions of higher learning. Should Esperanza try to convert her self-therapy into published content ("I put it down on paper and then the ghost does not ache so much"; 110), she could differentiate her work from that of her peers by converting her trauma into her creative "voice."

The force of McGurl's reading of the three mysterious women's "circle" emblematizes the self-referential "autopoetic circularity" that has been a primary feature of postwar literature (338). Readers can note how *Mango Street's* very narrative structure dramatizes the circularity of autopoiesis by not only looping its conclusion to its beginning but also explicitly linking this process to narration. "I like to tell stories," Esperanza states at the end of the novella in the vignette, "Mango Says Goodbye Sometimes." "I am going to tell you a story about a girl who didn't belong" (109). She then proceeds to recite the novella's opening line, thus, figuratively returning to the book's first vignette, "The House on Mango Street." The narrative loops back to its beginning, demonstrating how Esperanza becomes the author of *The House on Mango Street*.

Esperanza renders her experience and effectively writes herself into being. Her return to Mango Street need not be physical because she will textually revisit the site of her trauma. One could thus understand the novella's syntactically peculiar concluding sentence – "For the ones who cannot out" (110) – as exemplifying Esperanza's intervention. "Out," when used as a verb, indicates something becoming public (as in the phrase, "the truth will out"). Esperanza does not say she will help others "get out" of Mango Street; rather, she will help them "out" by placing their stories into circulation. What "coming back" for "the others" will look like, the ending implies, is the narrative testimony offered in the pages of the novella itself.

For McGurl, the voice Cisneros discovers while earning her MFA remains tied to "the authenticity of the ethnic voice" of her background (32), expressed in the "first-person form" of the short story-like vignettes cultivated in the University of Iowa's Writers' Workshop (339). The writer leaves her community only to self-reflexively return to it in the search for her emerging voice. In a valuable correction, Cutler shows how *Mango Street* dramatizes the emergence of Esperanza's *poetic* lyric subjectivity (131–133). Despite this difference, however, both he and McGurl agree that the *Mango Street* dramatizes the emergence of a writer who can form a bridge between her past (her ethnic background for McGurl, the women she leaves behind for Cutler) and her present status as a writer (her voice for McGurl, social critique for Cutler). The implications of their arguments suggest that the self-reflexive, self-making process of "autopoiesis," enabled by a university's creative writing program, gives the writer an opportunity to become herself while remaining true to who she already is. For a writer like Esperanza, this process would not only entail a way out of poverty (via the university) but also a way to represent a people (through fiction).

Readers get a poignant example of the implications of this dynamic in the vignette, "Minerva Writes Poems," in which the titular character appears trapped in a marriage with an alternatingly absent and abusive husband. As a way to cope, Minerva "writes poems on little pieces of paper that she folds over and over and holds in her hands a long time, little pieces of paper that smell like a dime" (84). Named after the Roman goddess of poetry, Minerva, and her poetic power remain immobilized. Her poems' dime-like smell alludes to their futility; she could write as many poems as she would like, but they would not make a dime's worth of difference. The vignette ends on a desperate note, with

Minerva showing up "black and blue," asking Esperanza, "what can she do." Esperanza's response continues the rhyme, "Minerva. I don't know which way she'll go. There is nothing *I* can do" (85; original emphasis). Esperanza's emphatic separation of herself from Minerva's situation suggests that it is Minerva who must leave the abusive marriage and somehow find the means to subsist. As Cutler explicates, however, the vignettes' embedded rhymes ("a long time," "like a dime"; "black and blue," "what can she do," "nothing *I* can do") suggest that *a poet* wrote them, a poetic narration that simultaneously highlights the difference and solidarity between Minerva the poet and the poetic voice describing her situation (140). For Cutler, the rhymes are a mark of the older Esperanza, now a poet, textually coming back for Minerva, narrating her story. He writes, "Poetry itself breaks through the surface [...] as it bears witness to Minerva's trauma [...] by speaking and witnessing, by *lyricising* Minerva's pain, Esperanza refuses its erasure" (140; original emphasis).

Yet Cutler does not acknowledge the contrast that the vignette itself makes clear: Insofar as it is poetry that can intervene on Minerva's behalf, it is not merely poetry as such but, rather, the poetry that is published and circulated. The difference between Minerva the poet and the poet Esperanza will become depends on the circulation enabled by institutional accreditation that acknowledges the drive toward creativity and expression. This accreditation could convert Esperanza's "personal experience" into the cultural capital that she might then use to help Minerva.

Indeed, even as it might understand itself as offering a "counter-discourse" (Cutler 121), *Mango Street* dramatizes the very policy recommendations offered by Glazer and Moynihan. They downplay the role of government and instead support the placement of people of color in leadership roles. "Conceivably," Glazer and Moynihan argue, "institutions organized, supported, and staffed by Negroes might be much more effective than the government and private agencies that now deal with these problems" (53). People of color in visible leadership roles could provide the otherwise missing models that others like them could follow. Glazer and Moynihan lament the absence of such a "self-help effort" in African American communities because the problem has become so pervasive that the black middle class did not see itself as a solution (53). In their view, the "American Negro" has not developed a "culture" that provides a sense of communal belonging and obligation. They repeat this diagnosis when highlighting Puerto Rico's "tiny upper class," which never demonstrated "signs of energetic leadership." They write, "Spanish cultural heritage was transmitted inadequately" to Puerto Ricans who had not developed a "network of culture, religion, art, [and] custom that gives strength and grace and meaning to a life of hardship" (87). In their assessment, some ethnicities are less equipped to become successful because they do not have the proper cultural guides that would help foster productive behavior. When Glazer and Moynihan consider the situation faced by overwhelmed Puerto Rican single mothers living in New York, their one note of optimism centers on "an impressive amount of activity by young, educated Puerto Ricans to raise the level of concern for education" (128). The educated, rising middle class can return to their neighborhoods and proselytize the advantages of education, demonstrating to overworked mothers and their children how they, too, could work hard, go to school, and help themselves.

Compare Glazer and Moynihan's assessment to what is shown in *Mango Street*. When Esperanza's mother advises her to become, in her words, "somebody" – "Esperanza, you go to school. Study hard" – she does so as a way to prevent Esperanza from becoming dependent on men who, in one form or another, always leave (91). The character Alicia has learned this lesson; she goes to college because she has learned to fear "four-legged fur. And fathers," the symptoms of poverty (including rats) and the perpetrators of patriarchy (a different kind of rat; 32). Alicia resents how she has "inherited her mama's [tortilla] rolling pin and sleepiness" (32). The death of Alicia's mother forces her to take her place, waking before sunrise to make her family's "lunchbox tortillas." This position is enforced by her father, who argues that "a woman's place is sleeping so she can wake up early with the tortilla star." Alicia takes "[t]wo trains and a bus" to attend a university and thereby avoid a "life in a factory or behind a rolling pin" (31–32). Through the character Alicia, the novella depicts higher education as a viable gateway to escape.

Although trying to better her station in life, however, Alicia remains on Mango Street and models what the three mysterious women mean by a "circle." Although she first appears in Esperanza's narrative as what Esperanza takes to be a source of condescension ("Alicia is stuck-up ever since she went to college"; 12), Alicia later appears as a source of information ("hips are scientific, I say repeating what Alicia already told me"; 50). These two quotations display Esperanza's naive misunderstanding, but also Alicia's guiding influence; not only is Alicia not "stuck up," but the text implies that she is trying to teach Esperanza something that goes far beyond how "scientific" women's hips are. The feedback loop comprising a cadre of those who can leave Mango Street counters the cycle of poverty and patriarchy that function to keep women in their "place" by providing a guiding model imparting the necessary information women need to know about their bodies and future. This is why Alicia helps Esperanza understand her role within the circuit. Although Esperanza resists the injunction that she should return to Mango Street "until somebody makes it better," Alicia – serving as a guiding influence – insists that Esperanza herself should become that somebody. "Who's going to do it?" she asks Esperanza, "The mayor?" At the mention of the mayor, Esperanza laughs because "the thought of the mayor coming to Mango Street" strikes her as ridiculous (107). Alicia, in short, depicts the role of the (ascending) middle class – above that of the state – as the engine of social change.

Just as Esperanza's family moved to the house on Mango Street to escape an apartment where "the water pipes broke and the landlord wouldn't fix them because the house was too old" (4), and just as Alicia wants to leave her family's apartment plagued by mice scurrying across "swollen floorboards nobody fixes" (31), Esperanza wants to leave Mango Street because it itself represents a situation that she perceives as fundamentally broken, one that negligent landlords and mayors will not fix, but she might. Esperanza will become the person who helps make Mango Street better (as suggested by Alicia) by becoming "somebody" through higher education (as suggested by her mother).

Readers could understand this dynamic via Glazer and Moynihan's perspective: The college graduate comes back and serves as a model for young girls, as the source of cultural capital, and as a producer of a cultural artifact that can become uplifting for women. Alternatively, readers could view this dynamic from Cutler's perspective: The writer testifies on behalf of women so that their experiences are not forgotten or misrepresented in facile characterizations of single motherhood. Both result in a practically homologous view of what could constitute a viable intervention. This homology explains why Cutler would argue that "it is no surprise that Cisneros has used her success to give other working-class and racialized writers opportunities for advancement and exposure, founding the Macondo Writing Workshop in 1995 and giving generously of her time and money" (136). He refers to a writer's workshop Cisneros started for marginalized writers "who view their work," as the Macondo Foundation's website puts it, "as part of a larger task of community-building." Cutler understands Cisneros' efforts as a continuation of her counternarrative and uses the work of sociologist Jody Agius Vallejo to make his case, stating, "Vallejo argues that this kind of solidarity is typical of Mexican Americans who have experienced upward mobility" (136). Vallejo calls this ethnic solidarity the "minority culture of mobility," which Cutler understands to be "a trenchant *critique* of the culture of poverty hypothesis" (136; emphasis added). The logic I have been tracking is on full display: Writers from struggling communities will make it out of those communities, attend a workshop, and then return to the communities to strengthen them. This return is precisely what Glazer and Moynihan would call "self-help."

Indeed, Agius Vallejo does not disagree with Glazer and Moynihan's perspective so much as she shows that their analysis does not apply to Mexican

Americans. Whereas Glazer and Moynihan might argue that some ethnicities have not established a robust culture that unites the efforts of the middle and lower classes, Vallejo highlights that there is, in fact, an abiding, proud culture that produces a sense of obligation within the disparate classes of the Mexican American community. Indeed, the policy recommendations she offers in *Barrios to Burbs* sometimes appear indistinguishable from those of *Beyond the Melting Pot*. She too advocates for the use of "middle-class mentors" who can, in her words, "infuse low-income Mexican American communities with different types of capital," including "social and human capital." Such mentors "not only show low-income youth what can be achieved, they actively help channel aspirations into reality because they fill the gaps in educational resources in families and schools" (186).

This narrative of self-help legitimizes the belief in meritocracy underlying the culture of poverty thesis by perpetuating the idea that positive images of the ascending middle class can function as motivating models, as sources of inspiration. This legitimizing story could not be any clearer than how it is mobilized in autobiographies like Robert Renteria's *From the Barrio to the Board Room: Reaching Out to Help Those Chasing the American Dream!* Renteria's overall messages are these: "Work hard" and, as the book's cover puts it, "Don't let where you came from dictate who you are, but let it be part of who you become." These platitudes highlight the circular logic of self-making that I have been analyzing and repeat the advice given to Esperanza by the three mysterious women: "You will always be Esperanza," they tell her. "You will always be Mango Street. You can't erase what you know. You can't forget who you are" (105). Who Esperanza (and those like her) should remember to be is what she should return to help fix, which she will do once she becomes herself by finding her voice. The circularity of this logic is reproduced in the dynamic of the intervention. Once one makes it to the board room, she should return to the barrio to help others make it out, too. Once one makes it to the writer's workshop, she should return to the barrio to mine its literary vein and circulate its stories. What Glazer and Moynihan might characterize as shameful, the pathology of one's background, is here translated into a source of pride, the origin of one's identity and voice.

The work that the novella's bildungsroman plot undertakes is the reinforcement of the link between the fate of the individual to those she leaves behind, even as that fate is guided by what can be characterized as self-interest. Although Esperanza feels "selfish" when the three women exhort her to come back because, at that moment, her justifiable desire to leave Mango Street registers as merely self-interested, part of the point of the novella – why Cisneros dedicates it to "The Women" – depends on Esperanza coming to understand her situation as representative of a pervasive problem. As the utterance of the three women's insistence shows, Esperanza's realization will be gradual; the more they insist that she return, the more specific their exhortation becomes ("come back [...] come back for the others [...] come back for the others who cannot leave [...]"; 105). Writing for oneself as a form of self-care, personal expression, and autopoetic self-making performs the function of social witnessing when the writer can identify the identity between her situation and that of those she represents. What she achieves for herself is thereby understood as an achievement for others.

To read *Mango Street* through the lens of McGurl's *Program Era*, then, is to understand the extent to which the novella is, as McGurl puts it, "heavily committed to the virtues of upward mobility," as it is invested in thematizing the "act of literary self-making" (338). *Mango Street* displays the deep homology between the "autopoetic circularity" of the program era's literature and the belief in "student enrichment through autonomous self-creation" that is at the heart of the promise of a higher education (McGurl 3). The novella's vignette titled, "A House of My Own," affirms this homology by articulating it via Esperanza's longing: "Only a house quiet as snow, a space for myself to go, clean as paper before the poem" (108). Whereas "paper" becomes the "bags" that Esperanza will pack when she leaves *Mango Street,* in this poetically expressed desire, "house" and "paper" metaphorically fuse as the enabling medium for poetry, which itself becomes the site of self-making. Cisneros affirms this symbolic homology in *A House of My Own* (2015), in which she describes, "A house. A writing machine. These two go hand in hand for me," thereby unifying the desire for a house and the desire to be a writer (6). *Mango Street* exemplifies a commitment to the promise of a flourishing life that is the goal of the American Dream – the independence enabled by property, the self-development enabled by education – such that the hope that Esperanza could connote ultimately affirms the belief that higher education can function as a crucial pathway to the middle class, even as the validity of this belief is increasingly difficult to maintain.

9 Against Literature? The Redistributive within *The House on Mango Street*

One might conclude that, as a novella, *Mango Street* cannot but exemplify the recognitional logic that undergirds a middle-class political vision of upward-class mobility. Recall Rodriguez's argument about the genre's role in the historical transition from feudalism to capitalism, "the relationship of the novel to the rise of the middle class in eighteenth-century Europe" (173).

Making a version of this history relevant for the United States and Latin American contexts, John Beverley's *Against Literature* (1993) describes how literature "had a central role in the self-representation of the upper and upper-middle strata of Latin American society; it was one of the social practices by which such strata constituted themselves as dominant" (ix). Stated in the broadest terms, novels have tended to support the politics of hegemonic maintenance. Given this history, it would seem that an organic intellectual within academia who wants to advocate on behalf of the poor would want to reform literary studies as it exists, or, as Beverley's title states, be *against literature*.

Yet even Rodriguez describes a redistributive possibility within the reading and teaching of literature. He narrates how, when he taught at Berkeley as a graduate student, he "lectured on Spenser or Dickens, insisting that the reader of literature is made mindful of his social position and privilege" (158). By "writing for a middle-class audience," argues Rodriguez, Charles Dickens makes his readers *aware* of their ability to effect social reform" (149; emphasis added). Such an awareness, I have argued, is what redistributive literature enables. So perhaps readers could similarly tease out within literary works such as *Mango Street* a redistributive strain, thereby cultivating this self-diagnostic skill.

Cisneros herself wonders what the role of teaching literature could be to help students living in precarious situations. "As a high school teacher," she writes, "I had no idea how to save my students from their own lives except to include them in my writing, not for their sake, but for my own. I couldn't undo myself from their stories any other way. How do you get any sleep at night if you witness stories that don't let you go" (*A House of My Own* 39). Like Esperanza, whose writing keeps the ghosts of her past at bay, Cisneros' psychic self-maintenance involves writing about the stories that haunt her sleep. Although Cisneros claims she was doing this "not for their sake, but for my own," her self-interested extrication mirrors the separation Esperanza must first experience (emphatically differentiating her situation from Minerva's, leaving the other woman on Mango Street) before fully asserting the solidarity of her writing with the women's plight. This type of writing, what I have been calling recognitional, enables this feeling of solidarity by seeking to bridge the gap between the writer and those about whom she writes.

Yet Cisneros' comments help make clear that what enables the therapeutic effect of her writing is artistic detachment, an extrication of the writer's stories from "their stories." One might characterize the distinction here much more generally as the difference between the work of the writer on the one hand and the facts of the world on the other. Cisneros' description offers a competing notion of writing, one that does not seek to overcome the difference between the writer and the depicted subject via the assertion of a common identity or the inducement of sympathy. Instead, this understanding of literature, what I have been calling redistributive, emphasizes the separation of "their stories" from "my writing" and establishes a critical perspective through which the affairs of the world could be evaluated, even as they are incorporated into the realm of art.

This distinct aesthetic mode animates a key moment in *Mango Street* wherein the reader is not asked to sympathize with its characters. The vignette, "There Was an Old Woman She Had So Many Children She Didn't Know What to Do," enacts the overwhelmed desperation of its old woman character with the near breathlessness of its title. Esperanza begins to relate this woman's situation sympathetically: "It's not her fault you know, except that she is their mother and only one against so many. They are bad those Vargases, and how can they help it with only one mother who is tired all the time [. . .] and who cries every day for the man who left without even leaving a dollar for bologna or a note explaining how come" (29). Esperanza's account underscores how the single mother does everything she can to subsist and, thus, should not be blamed for not working hard enough. The children's "badness" is not entirely their fault either. As Esperanza continues describing Old Lady Vargas' situation, however, her sympathy begins to wear thin. "But after a while you get tired of being worried about kids who aren't even yours," she confesses. "They are without respect for all things living, including themselves" (29). These observations are offered as asides to the reader, voiced with a tone of familiarity that comes at the observed children's expense: "See. That's what I mean. No wonder everybody gave up. Just stopped looking out [. . .]" (30). Esperanza assumes an observer's perspective external to the scene she describes, a position she invites her readers to inhabit.

However, readers distance themselves from the depicted scene and from Esperanza's assessment. Esperanza's exasperation, even if understandable, feels not quite right, especially in light of the vignette's conclusion, which depicts the death of one of the Vargas boys. Revealingly named "Angel," the boy is left unattended and "learned how to fly and dropped from the sky like a sugar donut [. . .] exploded down to earth without even an 'Oh'" (30). Readers could consider Angel's fall as either the inevitable outcome of the wicked (the figure of the "fallen angel") or a tragic injustice inflicted on the innocent (the boy as "angel"). Stated differently, readers can either blame the victim for his death or evaluate the situation leading to a tragedy that is neither his nor his mother's fault. The juxtaposition of the event and its soundless response helps adjudicate the interpretive ambiguity by highlighting the nonequivalence of a child's death and the reaction this death failed to elicit. This juxtaposition of the event and the lack of a response (not even an "Oh") exposes the incongruity between the narrative perspective (the judgmental exasperation) and what should be the stance regarding the events leading up to the death. Those witnessing the lives of the mother and her children should not merely sigh sympathetically nor shrug in frustration and impotence. They should not blame the victims for a situation beyond their control.

The critical distance between Esperanza and the reader thus facilitates the rejection of what some critics of Glazer and Moynihan describe as their "blame the victim" approach.[41] When Glazer and Moynihan describe the "disorganized families" of overwhelmed Puerto Rican mothers living in New York, for example, they write, "where the effort to raise [their children] in proper fashion has been given up, they are allowed to run wild!" (124). Because Puerto Rican mothers' lives do not conform to what the sociologists deem as "proper," these mothers simply "give up" and raise a generation of maladjusted (savage) children. Esperanza's judgmental criticism ("they are without respect") reproduces the condescension of Glazer and Moynihan's analysis ("they are allowed to run wild"). Yet for Cutler, the difference between *Mango Street* and *Beyond the Melting Pot* is one of point-of-view narration. For him, the sociologists present themselves as the supposed objective outsiders, whereas Cisneros presents Esperanza as a fully involved, sympathetic narrative voice describing the women's lives from within. Notice how Cutler's argument does not adequately explain this vignette's narration. Cisneros does not simply offer a counternarrative to the sociologists' account by, as Cutler argues, "dramatiz[ing] experiences of poverty and urban life from the inside out" (130). Rather, the novella critically reproduces the social scientists' "external" point of view. If, as Cutler argues, the sociologists' status as social scientists touts a degree of objectivity that their judgmental comments belie, the novelist's status as artist implies a commitment to subjectivity that *Mango Street* strategically exhausts.

The vignette dramatizes the insufficiency of sympathy, which depletes itself into exasperation and apathy. When devoid of an alternative situation for the recipients of the sympathy – devoid of, say, an influx of resources to help those like the old woman – sympathy devolves into moralism and condescension. By inviting readers not only to observe the Vargases through Esperanza's eyes but also to share her exasperated assessment of their situation, the vignette ultimately prompts readers to distinguish their conclusions from hers. The dramatic irony behind the exclamation, "they are without respect," calls into question the perspective that would look at this situation and see in the poor something like a conditioned sense of depravity. Instead, the vignette would have its readers see that what is depraved about the woman and her children is not them but their situation.

---

[41] See Blea's *Toward a Chicano Social Science.*

By adducing the writing of Brecht once more, we can productively unpack this distinction between a moral condemnation of character and a structural assessment of class. Describing his own exasperated mother character, Mother Courage, Brecht writes, "the depravity is not so much that of her person as that of her class" (*Mother* 114). Brecht invites the reader to consider the fundamental difference between their moral castigation of his character (as well as their sympathetic catharsis) and their understanding of the structural context that leads to the character's situation. Differentiating between "epic" and "dramatic" forms of theatrical storytelling, Brecht argues that the epic mode precludes the absorptive, sympathetic identification between characters and audience, a distinction he exemplifies by describing two ways of playing the titular role of his play, *Mother Courage*. "When the title role is played in the usual [dramatic] way, so as to communicate empathy," writes Brecht, "the spectator [...] experiences an extraordinary pleasure: the indestructible vitality of this woman beset by the hardships of war leaves him with a sense of triumph" (*Mother* 135–136). For Brecht, such a cathartic depiction would confirm the "bourgeois" audience's expectations by highlighting the "Niobe-like tragedy and the heart-rending vitality of all maternal creatures" (*Mother* 85). By celebrating a mother's unassailable love for her children in the face of all odds, the play would naturalize her situation, presenting it as an inescapable fate. Instead, Brecht's vision of what he calls "great art" displaces empathy in favor of having an audience exclaim, "I'd never have thought it – That's not the way – That's extraordinary, hardly believable – It's got to stop – The sufferings of this [wo]man appall me, because they are unnecessary – That's great art: nothing obvious in it – I laugh when they weep, I weep when they laugh" (*Brecht* 71). By differentiating the emotions of the audience from those of the characters, Brecht would have the audience see a situation of poverty "not as natural but as [...] belonging to a historical, transient period," subject to change and responsive to intervention (*Mother* 136).

Brecht is one of the most well-known proponents of the critical, redistributive approach to art I am teasing out in Cisneros's novella. Although my invocation of Brecht may appear as an unnecessary importation, Cisneros herself provides a way of considering Brecht as an organic feature of her development. She describes how, after she stopped teaching high school, she travelled to Europe, where she completed *Mango Street*. "Was I reading during this time?" she wonders, recalling her trip. "I know I had a paperback copy of *The Necessity of Art: A Marxist Approach* [1963] by Ernst Fischer [...] there are passages underlined only in early chapters, though I carried the book around with me through Greece, Italy, France, Spain, and Yugoslavia, trying to appear intelligent. I remember none of it" (*A House of My Own* 21). In those early chapters of

Fischer's text – the very first sentence of the book's very first page – Cisneros would have encountered the following quotation: "Poetry is indispensable – if only I knew what for" (7). For a young writer questioning how poetry might save women in peril, wondering what function literature serves, and questioning why literature should be taught to people living "desperate lives," the first line of Fischer's book might have been one she underlined, and *The Necessity of Art* could have provided one approach for finding the answers.

For Fischer, art's "raison d'être" changes to suit different historically emergent social needs (11). The "essential function" art must perform for "man" living under the conditions of capitalism needs to be that of "*enlightening and stimulating action*" (14; original emphasis), which is why Fischer quotes and paraphrases none other than Bertolt Brecht at every turn in his opening chapter: "The work of art must grip the audience not through passive identification but through an appeal to reason which demands action and decision" (10). The beholder, or reader, should be in a position to "pass judgment" in the face of a work of art. Quoting Brecht – using the very quotation I cited earlier – Fischer argues that the audience should be able to exclaim, "That's not the way to do it. This is very strange, almost unbelievable. This must stop" (11).

The House on Mango Street can thus be understood as demonstrating both the recognitional logic of McGurl's Program Era literature and the redistributive logic of Brechtian modernism. In its redistributive mode, the Esperanza appears not as a point of identification for the reader but as a character inscribed in a narrative. *Mango Street* highlights the character's status as a narrator whose first-person account the reader comes to understand as shortsighted.

But even as one could identify a redistributive strain within *Mango Street*, it ultimately collapses into a recognitional conclusion. As *Mango Street* reaches its culmination, the fundamental difference between the reader's perspective and Esperanza's understanding emotively collapses as readers see her emerging self-realization as triumphant. Going back to the vignette, "Minerva Writes Poems," although Esperanza emphatically abnegates her responsibility for Minerva ("There is nothing *I* can do"; 85; original emphasis), she will come to understand that there is something she can and should do.[42] She should become the credentialed writer who "comes back" for Minerva through Esperanza's writing. Contrast this conclusion to Brecht's *Mother Courage*, for

---

[42] Depicting poor women in need, Old Lady Vargas' and Minerva's vignettes are thematically related. Both vignettes echo the Mother Goose nursery rhyme about the old woman "who lived in a shoe / She had so many children, she didn't know what to do." Vargas and Minerva also do not know what to do with so many children they can barely support. Whereas the Mother Goose character feeds her children broth "without bread" before putting them to bed, Minerva feeds her children a "pancake dinner" before sending them to bed.

which "the bitterest and most meaningful lesson of the play" is the fact that the character, Mother Courage, "learned nothing from her misery [...] even at the end she does not *understand* " (*Mother* 137; original emphasis). But if, for Brecht, "It is not the playwright's job to open Courage's eyes at the end [...] his concern is with the eyes of the audience" (*Mother* 88), for Cisneros, Esperanza's eyes ultimately *are* the eyes of the audience. "One thing I know for certain," writes Cisneros in the novella's tenth anniversary preface, "you, the reader, are Esperanza. [...] You are Esperanza. You cannot forget who you are" (*A House of My Own* 131). For Cisneros' *Mango Street*, then, the narrative force driving the bildungsroman is one in which Esperanza must come to recognize the power of her intervention to help those she leaves behind.

In short, between an aesthetic of identification and sympathy (the recognitional) and one of artistic detachment and critique (the redistributive), *Mango Street* ultimately chooses the former, even as it provides a glimpse of the latter. A Brechtian aesthetic might have allowed for the reproduction of the narrative of midcentury sociology without capitulating to its arguments. Yet the novella's embodiment of the logic of autopoiesis collapses this potential critical distance, thereby reproducing the narrative of bootstrap upward mobility not as its critique but as its dramatized exemplification.

10 Conclusion: On Trying to Get It Right

By identifying this redistributive strain, *Race Class* might be misunderstood as offering a more concrete account of how the study of redistributive literature could cultivate an evaluative distance that enables causal understanding. I might be seen as offering a more specific description of what Joseph North wants: the cultivation, through literary study, of an oppositional perspective through which social assessment and political change are possible. For North, unless literature professors consider "using works of literature for the cultivation of aesthetic sensibility, with the goal of more general cultural and political change" (3), those on the political left, "cannot win" (xi). This understanding, however, is not what has motivated *Race Class*. Against North's account that a search for truth is motivated by one's political affiliations (x–xi), I offer instead an account that attempts to advance knowledge of the literary works in question without having to justify the attempt. By insisting that students and teachers of literature provide a political justification for their enterprise, one might implicitly agree with neoliberal accounts of value understood only in relation to market deliverables. In this view, one studies literature to do something else – and if they cannot do something else, why bother?

Insofar as readers can tease out a redistributive moment in a recognitional novella (as I did in *The House on Mango Street*), they can do so, perhaps, only to the extent that they already have a political view in mind prior to their reading of the novella. The novella would not shock them out of their complacency so much as it would reinforce a political view they already have. Literature, in this view, essentially supplies case studies to be examined for their political self-affirmation and their proselytizing utility. If the point of what one does is to "win," as North argues (xi), what professors of literature do when teaching is use literary case studies to teach students to think as they do: Literary studies understood as political indoctrination.

What motivated my writing of *Race Class*, however, has been the sense that literary critics and historians have gotten something fundamentally wrong about twentieth-century literature and history, and critics and professors of literature keep making this mistake when thinking about the politics this literature enables. My goal, then, has been to clarify our understanding of the texts, not to project my political beliefs onto them nor to affirm my biases. My readings may be shortsighted and limited, of course. I may have misread the texts I have heretofore claimed to clarify. I welcome my readers to highlight these limitations and to disagree with my readings. We can interpretively disagree because the meaning of the texts is not a projection of my or your desires or opinions. The meaning of these texts remains formally embodied despite my biases and yours. Interpretive disagreement comes with the territory when there is a normative truth at stake, "normative" because we can indeed be mistaken about the textually embodied meaning.

I am, then, not interested in legislating anyone's relationship to neoliberalism. I am not trying to change how anyone votes. I am instead invested in producing an accurate account of the texts in question so that, insofar as instructors and literary critics insist on turning to literature to advance their politics, we will have a better account of what politics have been advanced.

Works Cited

Appiah, Kwame Anthony. *In My Father's House: Africa in the Philosophy of Culture*. Oxford University Press, 1992.
Aranda, Jóse. *When We Arrive: A New Literary History of Mexican America*. University of Arizona Press, 2003.
Arellano, José Antonio. 'The Borders of the Frame': Chicanx Feminism and the Problem of Representation. *Forma*, vol. 1, no. 2, 2020, pp. 35–62.
Ashton, Jennifer. "Poetry and the Price of Milk." *Nonsite.Org*, September 13, 2013, nonsite.org/poetry-and-the-price-of-milk/.
Auletta, Ken. *The Underclass*. Overlook Press, 1999.
Beverley, John. *Against Literature*. University of Minnesota Press, 1993.
Beverley, John. *Testimonio: On the Politics of Truth*. University of Minnesota Press, 2004.
Blea, Irene I. *Toward A Chicano Social Science*. Praeger, 1988.
Brecht, Bertolt. *Brecht on Theatre: The Development of an Aesthetic*. Edited by John Willett, Hill and Wang, 1992.
Brecht, Bertolt. *Mother Courage and Her Children*. Penguin Books, 2008.
Broyles-González, Yolanda. *El Teatro Campesino Theater in the Chicano Movement*. University of Texas Press, 1994.
Bruenig, Matt. "The Racial Wealth Gap Is About the Upper Classes." *Jacobin*, July 5, 2020, https://jacobin.com/2020/07/racial-wealth-gap-redistribution.
Bui, Quoctrung. "The Fall and Rise of U.S. Inequality, in 2 Graphs." *NPR*, NPR, February 11, 2015, www.npr.org/sections/money/2015/02/11/384988128/the-fall-and-rise-of-u-s-inequality-in-2-graphs.
Burgos, Elizabeth. "How I Became Persona Non Grata." In *Rigoberta Menchú and the Story of All Poor Guatemalans*, edited by David Stoll, Routledge, 2008, ix–xvii.
Chicano: From Caricature to Self-Portrait. Edited by Edward R. Simmen, Signet, 1971.
Cisneros, Sandra. *A House of My Own*. Knopf Doubleday Publishing Group, 2015.
Cisneros, Sandra. *The House on Mango Street*. Vintage Books, 1984.
Collini, Stefan. "Exaggerated Ambitions: The Case for Studying Literature." *London Review of Books*, vol. 44, no. 23, December 2022. www.lrb.co.uk/the-paper/v44/n23/stefan-collini/exaggerated-ambitions.
Cowie, Jefferson. *Stayin' Alive: The 1970s and the Last Days of the Working Class*. The New Press, 2010.

Cutler, John Alba. *Ends of Assimilation: The Formation of Chicano Literature.* Oxford University Press, 2015.

Dávila, Arlene M. *Latinx Art: Artists, Markets, Politics.* Duke University Press, 2020.

Di Stefano, Eugenio Claudio. *The Vanishing Frame: Latin American Culture and Theory in the Postdictatorial Era.* University of Texas Press, 2021.

D'Souza, Dinesh. *Illiberal Education: The Politics of Race and Sex on Campus.* The Free Press, 1991.

Dunn, John Gregory. "The Secret of Danny Santiago." *New York Review of Books*, August 16, 1984.

Dyson, Michael Eric. "Haley's Comet." *Roots*, by Alex Haley, Vanguard Books, 2007.

Edmonson, Munro. *Los Manitos: A Study of institutional Values.* Middle American Research Institute, 1957.

Felstiner, John, and Pablo Neruda. *Translating Neruda: The Way to Macchu Picchu.* Stanford University Press, 1980.

Fields, Karen E., and Barbara J. Fields. *Racecraft: The Soul of Inequality in American Life.* Verso, 2012.

Findeisen, Christopher. "Injuries of Class: Mass Education and the American Campus Novel." *PMLA*, vol. 130, no. 3, March 2015, pp. 284–298. *JSTOR*, www.jstor.org/stable/44015711.

Fischer, Ernst. *The Necessity of Art: A Marxist Approach.* Penguin Books, 1970.

Fish, Stanley. *Save the World on Your Own Time.* Oxford University Press, 2008.

Fraser, Nancy, and Axel Honneth. *Redistribution or Recognition: A Political-Philosophical Exchange.* Verso, 2003.

Frazier, Edward Franklin. *The Negro Family.* New York: Arno, 1968.

García, Mario T., and Sal Castro. *Blowout!: Sal Castro and the Chicano Struggle for Educational Justice.* University of North Carolina Press, 2014.

Glasgow, Douglas G. *Black Underclass.* Vintage Books, 2009.

Glazer, Nathan, and Daniel P. Moynihan. *Beyond the Melting Pot: The Negroes, Puerto Ricans, Jews, Italians, and Irish of New York City.* MIT Press, 1970.

Gómez-Quiñones, Juan. "Toward a Concept of Culture." *Revista Chicano-Riqueña*, vol. 5, no. 2, 1977, 29–44.

Gómez-Quiñones, Juan. *Chicano Politics: Reality and Promise, 1940–1990.* University of New Mexico Press, 1990.

Gómez-Quiñones, Juan, and Irene Vásquez. *Making Aztlán: Ideology and Culture of the Chicana and Chicano Movement, 1966–1977.* University of New Mexico Press, 2014.

González, Marcial. *Chicano Novels and the Politics of Form: Race, Class, and Reification.* University of Michigan Press, 2009.

Gramsci, Antonio. *Selections from the Prison Notebooks of Antonio Gramsci.* Edited and translated by Q. Hoare and G. N. Smith, International Publishers, 1971.

Gramsci, Antonio. "The Intellectuals." In *Contemporary Sociological Thought*, edited by Sean Pattrick Hier, Canadian Scholars' Press, 2005.

Guillory, John. *Cultural Capital: The Problem of Literary Canon Formation.* University of Chicago Press, 1993.

Guillory, John. *Professing Criticism: Essays on the Organization of Literary Study.* University of Chicago Press, 2022.

Haley, Alex. *Roots.* Vanguard Books, 2007.

Harth, Dorothy E., and Lewis M. Baldwin, editors. *Voices of Aztlan: Chicano Literature of Today.* New American Library, 1974.

Heller, Celia Stopnicka. *Mexican American Youth: Forgotten Youth at the Crossroads.* Random House, 1969.

Hernández, Deluvina. "La Raza Satellite System." *Aztlan*, vol. 1, no. 1, spring 1970.

Hinojosa, Rolando. "Mexican-American Literature: Toward an Identification." In *The Identification and Analysis of Chicano Literature*, ed. Francisco Jimenez, Tempe: Bilingual Press/Editorial Bilingue, 1979, 7–18.

Hinojosa, Rolando. *The Valley: Estampas Del Valle.* Arte Público Press, 2014.

Hurtado, Sylvia. "Trend Analyses from 1971 to 2012 on Mexican American/Chicano Freshmen:Are We Making Progress?" In *The Magic Key: The Educational Journey of Mexican Americans from K–12 to College and Beyond*, edited by Ruth Enid Zambrana and Sylvia Hurtado, University of Texas Press, 2015, pp. 53–75.

Hurtado, Sylvia, Victor B. Saenz, José Luis Santos, and Nolan L. Cabrera. *Advancing in Higher Education: A Portrait of Latina/o College Freshmen at Four-Year Institutions, 1975–2006.* Higher Education Research Institute, University of California, Los Angeles, 2007.

Islas, Arturo. *The Rain God.* Alexandrian, 1984.

Islas, Arturo. *Migrant Souls: A Novel.* Morrow, 1990.

Lewis, Oscar. *Five Families: Mexican Case Studies in the Culture of Poverty.* Basic Books, 1959.

Lewis, Oscar. *La Vida: A Puerto Rican Family in the Culture of Poverty – San Juan and New York.* Random House, 1966.

Madsen, William. *The Mexican Americans of South Texas.* Holt, Rinehart and Winston, 1964.

McGurl, Mark. *The Program Era: Postwar Fiction and the Rise of Creative Writing.* Harvard University Press, 2009.

Mead, Lawrence M. *Beyond Entitlement.* Free Press, 2014.

Michaels, Walter Benn. "Race Into Culture: A Critical Genealogy of Cultural Identity." *Critical Inquiry*, vol. 18, no. 4, summer 1992, pp. 655–685.

Michaels, Walter Benn. "The Political Economy of Anti-Racism." *No Politics but Class Politics*, edited by Anton Jager and Daniel Zamora, Eris, 2022, pp. 101–114.

Muñoz, Carlos. *Youth, Identity, Power: The Chicano Movement*. Verso, 2007.

Navarrette, Rubén. *A Darker Shade of Crimson: Odyssey of a Harvard Chicano*. Bantam Books, 1993.

Nelson, Cary, and Lawrence Grossberg. *Marxism and the Interpretation of Culture*. University of Illinois Press, 1988.

North, Joseph. *Literary Criticism: A Concise Political History*. Harvard University Press, 2017.

Ortego y Gasca, Philip D. *We Are Chicanos: An Anthology of Mexican-American Literature*. Washington Square, 1973.

Penalosa, Fernando. "Toward an Operational Definition of the Mexican American." *Aztlan*, vol. 1, no. 1, spring 1970.

¡Printing the Revolution!: The Rise and Impact of Chicano Graphics, 1965 to Now. Edited by E. Carmen Ramos, Smithsonian American Art Museum, 2020.

Reed, Jr., Adolph L. *Stirrings in the Jug: Black Politics in the Post-Segregation Era*. University of Minnesota Press, 1999.

Reed, Jr., Adolph L. *Class Notes: Posing as Politics and Other Thoughts on the American Scene*. New Press, 2000, vii–xxviii.

Riesman, David, and Nathan Glazer. *The Lonely Crowd: A Study of the Changing American Character*. 1950, repr. New Haven: Yale University Press, 2001.

Renteria, Robert, and Corey Blake. *From the Barrio to the Board Room: Reaching Out to Help Those Chasing the American Dream!* Writers of the Round Table Press, 2011.

The Rigoberta Menchú Controversy. Edited by Arturo Arias, University of Minnesota Press, 2001.

Rivera, Jaime Sena. "Chicanos: Culture, Community Role – Problems of Evidence, and a Proposition of Norms Towards Establishing Evidence." *Aztlan*, vol. 1, no. 1, spring 1970.

Rivera, Tomás. "Into the Labyrinth: The Chicano in Literature." In *Tomas Rivera: The Complete Works*, edited by Julián Olivares, Arte Publico Press, 2008, 325–337.

Rivera, Tomás. "Richard Rodriguez' *Hunger of Memory* as Humanistic Antithesis." In *Tomas Rivera: The Complete Works*, edited by Julián Olivares, Arte Publico Press, 2008, 406–414.

Rivera, Tomás. *. . . y no se lo trago la tierra*. Arte Publico Press, 1996.

Robbins, Bruce. *Criticism and Politics: A Polemical Introduction*. Stanford University Press, 2022.

Rodriguez, Richard. *Hunger of Memory: The Education of Richard Rodriguez: An Autobiography*. Dial Press, 2005.

Romano-V, Octavio Ignacio. "The Anthropology and Sociology of the Mexican-Americans." *El Grito*, vol. 2, 1968, pp. 13–26.

Santiago, Danny. "Danny Santiago Makes a Call on Daniel James." *Los Angeles Times,* August 15, 1984.

Santiago, Danny. *Famous All Over Town*. Plume, 1984.

Schneider, Alison. *Stanford Revisits the Course That Set off the Culture Wars*, www.chronicle.com/article/stanford-revisits-the-course-that-set-off-the-culture-wars/.

Simmen, Edward R. *Chicano: From Caricature to Self-Portrait*. Signet, 1971.

Stanford, Phil. "Roots and Grafts on the Haley Story." *Washington Star*, April 8, 1979.

Staten, Henry. "Ethnic Authenticity, Class, and Autobiography: The Case of Hunger of Memory." *PMLA*, vol. 113, no. 1, 1998, pp. 103–116.

Stein, Judith. *The Pivotal Decade*. Yale University Press, 2010.

Stoll, David. *Rigoberta Menchú and the Story of All Poor Guatemalans*. Routledge, 2008.

Striffler, Steve. *Solidarity: Latin America and the US Left in the Era of Human Rights*. Pluto Press, 2019.

Valdez, Luis. "Los Vendidos." In *Luis Valdez: Early Works: Actos, Bernabe, and Pensamiento Serpentino*, Arte Publico Press, 1990, 40–52.

Villarreal, José Antonio. *Clemente Chacón*. Bilingual Press, 1984.

Villarreal, José Antonio. *Pocho*. Anchor, 1989.

Voices of Aztlan: Chicano Literature of Today. Edited by Dorothy E. Harth and Lewis M. Baldwin, New American Library, 1974.

Wilson, William Julius. *The Truly Disadvantaged: The Inner City, the Underclass, and Public City*. University of Chicago Press, 1990.

Wright, Richard. *Black Boy: (American Hunger): A Record of Childhood and Youth*. Harper Perennial Modern Classics, 1998.

Wright, Richard. *Native Son*. Harper Perennial, 2005.

Yúdice, George. "*Testimonio* and Postmodernism." In *The Real Thing: Testimonial Discourse and Latin America*, edited by Georg M. Gugelberger. Duke University Press, 1996, 42–57.

Zamora, Daniel. "When Exclusion Replaces Exploitation: The Condition of the Surplus Population Under Neoliberalism." *Nonsite*, September 13, 2013, http://nonsite.org/feature/when-exclusion-replaces-exploitation#foot_src_8_6493.

Cambridge Elements

Race in American Literature and Culture

John Ernest
University of Delaware
John Ernest, the Judge Hugh M. Morris Professor and Chair of the Department of English at the University of Delaware, is the author of over 45 essays and author or editor of thirteen books, including *Liberation Historiography: African American Writers and the Challenge of History, 1794–1861* (2004), *Chaotic Justice: Rethinking African American Literary History* (2009), *The Oxford Handbook of the African American Slave Narrative* (2014), and *Race in American Literature and Culture* (2022).

Stephanie Li
Duke University
Stephanie Li is professor of English and African and African American Studies at Duke University. She has published seven books including the award-winning, *Something Akin to Freedom: The Choice of Bondage in Narratives by African American Women* (2010) as well as *Signifying without Specifying: Racial Discourse in the Age of Obama* (2011), *Playing in the White: Black Writers, White Subjects* (2015), and *Signifyin(g) Immigrants: Twenty-First Century Pan-African American Literature* (2018). She has also written two short biographies of Toni Morrison and Zora Neale Hurston. Her most recent book from the University of Minnesota Press is entitled *Ugly White People: Whiteness in Contemporary American Literature*. She is the editor of Volume E of *The Norton Anthology of American Literature, 11th edition* and the co-editor of the Cambridge University Press Series, "Race in US Literature and Culture." She has co-edited several special issues of *American Literary History and Black Camera*.

About the Series
The complex history of race shapes virtually every aspect of US politics and cultural life, and efforts to address both the challenges and the possibilities of US racial history are often marked by misinformation or misunderstanding. This series takes aim at the conventional wisdom, working towards a reconsidered past and a reimagined future.

Cambridge Elements⁼

Race in American Literature and Culture

Elements in the Series

Race Class: Reading Mexican American Literature in the Era of Neoliberalism, 1981–1984
José Antonio Arellano

A full series listing is available at: www.cambridge.org/ERAL

Printed by Integrated Books International,
United States of America